TEAM FITNESS

Also available from ASQ Quality Press

Management by Policy: How Companies Focus Their Total Quality Efforts to Achieve Competitive Advantage
Brendan Collins and Ernest Huge

Managing the Process, the People, and Yourself
Joseph G. Werner

Excellence Is a Habit: How to Avoid Quality Burnout
Thomas J. Barry

Reengineering the Organization: A Step-by-Step Approach to Corporate Revitalization
Jeffrey N. Lowenthal

Quality: The Ball in Your Court, 2nd Edition
Frank C. Collins, Jr.

Mapping Work Processes: A Guide for Self-Directed Teams
Dianne Galloway

The Way of Strategy
William A. Levinson

To request a complimentary catalog of publications, call 800-248-1946.

TEAM FITNESS

A How-To Manual for Building a Winning Work Team

Meg Hartzler

Jane E. Henry, Ph.D.

ASQ Quality Press
Milwaukee, Wisconsin

Team Fitness: A How-To Manual for Building a Winning Work Team
Meg Hartzler and Jane E. Henry, Ph.D.

Library of Congress Cataloging-in-Publication Data

Hartzler, Meg
    Team fitness: a how-to manual for building a winning work team/
  Meg Hartzler, Jane E. Henry.
      p.   cm.
    Includes bibliographical references and index.
    ISBN 0-87389-269-0
    1. Work groups.   I. Henry, Jane E.   II. Title.
  HD66.H375   1994
  658.4'02—dc20   93-48626
                                             CIP

10 9 8 7 6 5

ISBN 0-87389-269-0

Acquisitions Editor: Susan Westergard
Project Editor: Kelley Cardinal
Production Editor: Annette Wall
Marketing Administrator: Mark Olson
Set in Berkeley and Stone Sans by Montgomery Media, Inc.
Cover design by Montgomery Media, Inc.
Printed and bound by BookCrafters, Inc.

ASQC Mission: To facilitate continuous improvement and increase customer satisfaction by identifying, communicating, and promoting the use of quality principles, concepts, and technologies; and thereby be recognized throughout the world as the leading authority on, and champion for, quality.

For a free copy of the ASQC Quality Press Publications Catalog, including ASQC membership information, call 800-248-1946.

Printed in the United States of America

 Printed on acid-free recycled paper

American Society for Quality

Quality Press
611 East Wisconsin Avenue
P.O. Box 3005
Milwaukee, Wisconsin 53201-3005

Contents

Foreword ix

Acknowledgments xi

Introduction xiii

    The Challenge xiii

    How to Use This Manual xvi

Part 1 The Fitness Model 1

    Fitness Area 1: Customer Focus 4

    Fitness Area 2: Direction 5

    Fitness Area 3: Understanding 6

    Fitness Area 4: Accountability 7

Part 2 The Fitness Meter 9

    Characteristics of Effective Teams 11

    Beginners, Intermediates, Experts 13

    The Fitness Meter 14

    Fitness Meter Score Sheet 19

    Fitness Planning 24

Part 3 The Exercises 27

    Fitness Area I: Customer Focus Exercises 29

        1. Who Is the Customer 32

        2. Primary Customer Identification 34

        3. Customer Feedback and Measures 39

        4. Customer Priorities 41

        5. What Do Our Customers Want and Expect from Us? 46

        6. Moments of Truth 48

7. Moments of Truth Map 51
8. Customer Site Visits 55
9. Focus Groups for Internal or External Customers 60
10. Surveys 67
11. Tracking the Work 73
12. Walk a Mile in My Shoes 76

Fitness Area II: Direction Exercises 79
1. Project or Task Team New Team Charter 84
2. Long-Term or Ongoing Team Chartering Meeting...............89
3. A One-Day Visioning Meeting 94
4. Warm-Up Vision 97
5. Creating a Team Vision—with Pictures 99
6. Mission Statement 103
7. Short Mission Statement 108
8. Goals and Objectives Top-Down 114
9. Bottom-Up Goal Setting 118
10. Which Goals Have Priority? 121

Fitness Area III: Understanding Exercises 127
1. In-Depth Intros 130
2. What Makes Us Tick? 136
3. How Do I Use My Time? 139
4. Are We a Team or a Work Group? 143
5. Observing Individual Behaviors in Teamwork....................146
6. Consensus Decision Making 152
7. What Sport? 157
8. Ten-Minute Team Process 162
9. Process Check..165
10. Box and Bubble 167
11. Leadership Transition Meeting..170
12. Best Boss..174
13. Culture Audit 177
14. Culture Observation 181

Fitness Area IV: Accountability Exercises 185
1. Values Statements 190
2. If—Then—Then..194
3. Operating Agreements 197
4. Negotiating Ground Rules 201
5. Individual Contracting 203
6. Team Responsibility Chart 207

    7. ABC Priorities 211
    8. Implementation Responsibility Chart...................214
    9. Stakeholder Support 217
  10. Critical Success Factors 219

Appendices

  Appendix A—Types of Teams.......................................223
  Appendix B—New Team Start-Up 225
  Appendix C—How to Begin with an Existing Team...........227
  Appendix D—Teams and Time 229
  Appendix E—Planning an Off-Site Team Fitness Session...........231
  Appendix F—Roles and Tasks of a Facilitator..................235
  Appendix G—Use of Flip Charts 237

Index..241

Foreword

The modern organization has arrived! Instead of building on individual competencies and roles, it is built on teams. Teams are central to all types of organizational processes, ranging from customer relationships to quality efforts to cycle time reductions to manufacturing excellence. Knowing the importance of teams and being able to effectively use teams are two different issues.

Team Fitness is one of the most practical, useful, and valuable guidebooks to making teams work. The book is about doing, not talking; about making teams more fit, not providing theory about teams; about concrete actions for teamwork, not abstract ideals. The four steps to fitness (customer focus, direction, understanding, and accountability) represent the building blocks of effective teams. The exercises and tools in the book provide every manager from the senior executive to the first line supervisor with practical ways to make teams more effective.

Managers should not just read this book, but use and digest it. If the exercises are followed, managers will build more healthy organizations. It is a diet most managers cannot live without.

Dave Ulrich
Clinical Professor, School of Business Administration
University of Michigan

Acknowledgments

Writing this book has consumed a good portion of our time and energy. Thank goodness we had support, editing, help, and inspiration from many others. These are the people we want to thank.

Our colleagues at Destra, Dr. Pamela Dennis and Laurie Dodd, found time when there was none to do in-depth editing and input in many areas. Destra assistants Ruth Eastman and Shawna Lechuga organized the word processing and kept calm when we were not.

Other invaluable editors include Jan Swartz, Meg's sister, principal of Burkholder Middle School, Las Vegas, Nevada; Steen Jensen, principal, High 5 Consulting, formerly with Northern Telecom; William J. Martin, turnaround CEO; Maurice (Moe) Russell, vice-president of branch lending in four midwestern states, Farm Credit Services of the Midlands; Dr. Dodds Buchanan, marketing professor, University of Colorado; and Reg Gupton, realtor and trainer.

Some people encouraged us and took the model to the test of their team situations. They are Ken Lichtenstein, Susan Walden, Kit Connelly, Karen Regg, and Tim Fidler of GE Plastics, and Marvin Hass and his self-directed work teams in Farm Credit Services of Southeast Kansas.

Support and encouragement also came from Jane's colleagues at the Farm Credit Council including Kurt Ronsen and Michael Hotz, who also edited; Rosalie Holen, who helped with sanity and organization; Dean Lehman, Roger Shaffer, Connie McAndrews, and Crystal Munday-White, who gave moral support.

Our Vision

Our vision for this book-writing project was to use our best thinking and experiences to put together a manual that is readable, practical, personal, straightforward, and takes the mystery out of how to build an effective team.

Our vision for its use is that this text will become dog-eared, coffee-stained, and yellow highlighted, with its corners folded down, and falling open naturally to certain pages.

Jane and Meg

Others who lived through the pushes and deadlines side-by-side with us were Dale and Jeff Hartzler; Kristen and Kevin McCormick; David and Elise Hoerath; Claire Lindgren; Dorcas Murray; Bruce Jacobson, Larry Rosen, Ed Webster, Jordan Campbell, and Meg's partners, Pam and Laurie.

Marvin Weisbord and David Ulrich provided inspiration to Jane. Meg appreciates Eileen Morgan and Sandra Hirsh who pushed her to write.

Mary Lou Egan was our gracious, conscientious, and clever illustrator, whose drawings helped enliven the pages.

Thanks to the people who let us use their visions and values—Dave Woolfolk, Jim Styck, Rolf Haugen, and Mike Davis.

Especially, we want to thank the countless teams we have worked with over the past years, those with which we consulted, participated in, and led. Truly, we could not have done it without you. Thanks!

Good luck with your teams!

Introduction

THE CHALLENGE

- Bill Rogers' department has just been asked to be a pilot site for the company's new quality program.

- Engineer, Mark Garcia, received a memo today appointing him to a cross-functional work team.

- Elaine Watson is charged with determining the causes of variance on her assembly line.

- George Swartz is promoted to manage an existing work group.

- Donna Yamamoto wants to renew and invigorate her work team.

- Jim Jeffries is the new chairman of the board of directors of United Way.

> **Teamwork Trend**
>
> Self-directed teams have been empowered with responsibility for all functions at companies like Steelcase, Northern Telecom, and Johnsonville foods. Results from Northern Telecom Morrisville factory: revenue increase–63%; sales–26%; quality–50%; productivity per employee–60%; earnings–46%.
>
> J. Schidler, "Work Teams Boost Productivity," *Personnel Journal*, February 1992, 67–71.

As the reader, you probably selected this book because you are interested in the possibilities of building a team in your workplace. This process is happening throughout the United States and the world. Today, as never before, front-line supervisors, managers at all levels, and leaders in all kinds of organizations are being called upon to build teams to meet their companies' unique needs. Teams are required to produce quality products and services for today's competitive environment.

Everyone is part of one or more teams. Roles shift as individuals move from one team to another. One may be the leader of a business unit at work and a member of a task team for the chamber of commerce in the evening. People may lead a group at church, a favorite nonprofit organization, or their children's school, in addition to the work teams of which they are part every day. Our lives are touched by teamwork, or the lack of it, at every turn.

The challenge.

Some teams and leaders work on the fitness of their teams intuitively. They may or may not be able to explain what they did or how they did it. This book is for the teams and leaders who want a blueprint of activities, an overall plan to improve their teamwork.

Teamwork makes bottom-line sense, but you need to know where and how to start.

When you and your team are fit, you will be rewarded by the synergy and pride that comes as team member energy is released. Creative team decisions will blossom and you will gain focus and commitment to the team and the organization. You will see the results.

Teamwork *is* rewarding and exciting!

This book is a guide to help you develop a strategy and plan for your team. It is a step-by-step approach to diagnosing the team's needs, planning for team activities, and carrying out those activities.

Four major areas are key to developing a systematic approach to achieving successful team performance. The activities and exercises of *Team Fitness* are organized around the following four areas:

1. *Customer focus*—Shape your products and services by identifying your primary customers and clarifying their needs and expectations.
2. *Team direction*—Create a vision for your team, define your unique mission, and gain a shared purpose.
3. *Understanding*—Identify individual team member strengths and blind spots. Find ways to understand and support each other and strategies for effective teaming. Make sure your team can get things done in the organization.
4. *Accountability*—Build agreement on "who does what around here;" develop team operating principles; and clarify values.

> **A** regional sales manager frequently found himself helping his sales people see the need to team.
>
> In their discussions, he would use an analogy that comes from the notion of Best Ball golf. A scratch golfer often can shoot par (72) or better. Playing Best Ball, the foursome can score in the 60s consistently.
>
> His challenge to his people, "How do we play Best Ball in sales?"

Team Fitness is based on research, theory, and the authors' years of experience as members, leaders, and consultants to teams. This text provides the framework and exercises that are the essential elements for your team fitness program. In this manual you will find pragmatic, simple techniques and activities to raise your levels of productivity, profitability, and commitment.

Building a team is an ongoing process. Just as achieving optimum physical fitness requires dedication and training and practice, so does building a team. Any team can make improvements by choosing exercises that are short and straightforward, and then moving to more lengthy, tougher ones. Setting aside the time to focus on teamwork—to work out on a regular basis—is a requirement. *Team Fitness* will help you develop your own personalized plan and exercise schedule to get team fit.

Building a team is an ongoing process.

What a group of visitors found when they went to GE's Business Information Center in Albany, New York, was paradoxical. For example,

- Productivity up 106 percent in three years. Cost per customer down 46 percent
- Employees who gave the impression they were in charge, but gave their manager high marks
- This transformation being accomplished in a service enterprise, not in manufacturing, where such known gains had more frequently been achieved

In a two-year period this business transferred ownership of the business to the employees and became a self-directed work team. They used a structured process of letting go of control to strengthen their worldwide position of leadership.

James Burnside, *Letting Go*, General Electric Company, 1992.

HOW TO USE THIS MANUAL

This book is a manual, a how-to book. It is designed for you and your team to use on your own.

Step 1. Read the fitness model section.

Step 2. Leaf through the entire workbook to understand the variety of exercises available.

Step 3. Assess your current fitness level. Take the Team Fitness Meter yourself. Give the Team Fitness Meter to the other members of your team. Score your Team Fitness Meter. Examine the results with your team.

Step 4. Develop a fitness plan and a workout schedule that allow for a steady pace to build the strength of your team over time.

The sequence of activities will vary according to factors such as how long the team has been together, scope of responsibilities; the culture of the enterprise. The format of the activities is similar to that of a physical workout, with an exercise plan, a warmup, aerobics, and a cooldown.

You may copy any pages that are titled *Information Sheet* or *Worksheet* to make it easy for all your team to participate. (Permission is granted only for your own team's use.)

part one

THE FITNESS MODEL

A Four-Part Model

Effective teams are necessary to meet today's challenging business environment. In the competitive 90s, it is critical to unleash the power and creativity of all individuals to work toward the organization's goals. Teams need involvement from all members, they must be self directing on their key tasks, and must receive some support and guidance. For this to become a reality, teams must find the ways to work at their best.

To navigate through complex situations, conflicting demands, and limited resources, teams need fitness training and the tools to get things done. As shown in Figure 1.1, the four areas of team exercises and activities that help the team get fit are

- Customer focus

- Direction

- Understanding

- Accountability

Just as everyone knows it takes focus and commitment to maintain fitness through exercise, diet, and good habits, the team must dedicate time and energy to strengthen itself in each of these four areas. Let us examine these four fitness areas.

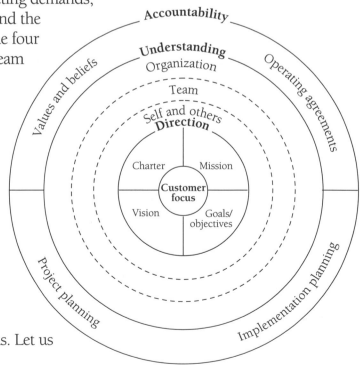

Figure 1.1. Team fitness.

FITNESS AREA 1: CUSTOMER FOCUS

Definition: Customer focus is getting clear on the expectations, values, and priorities of those who receive your work, and ensuring that those expectations shape the requirements for the products and services you provide.

Factors: Customer focus has two parts: identification of customers, and clarification of the customers' requirements and expectations.

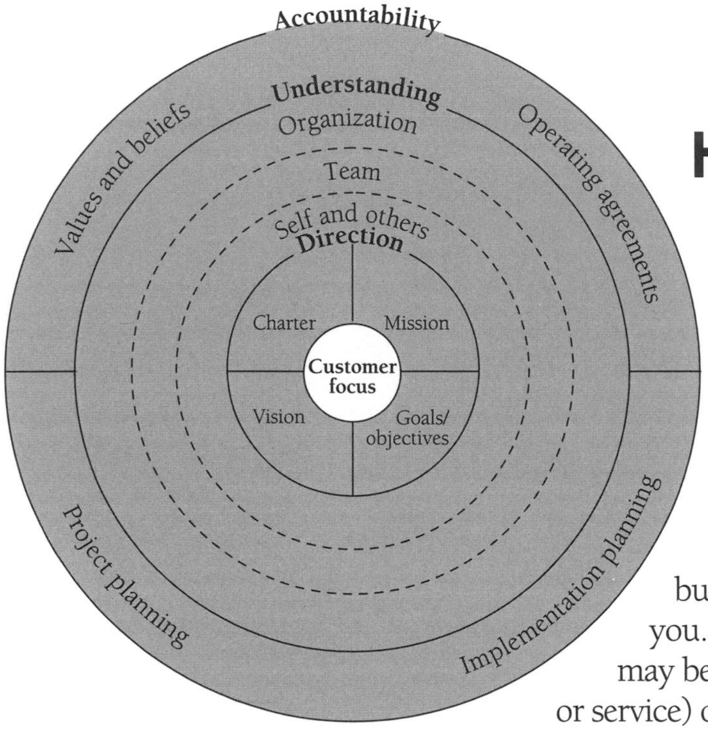

How focusing on the customer contributes to team fitness

Customer focus is the heart of the fitness plan (Figure 1.2). The voice of each customer must be heard throughout the company. Everyone must understand the customer's needs and expectations, so that every decision is made with an eye on the impact it may have on the customer.

Customers come in all shapes and sizes, from a kid buying a hamburger to the person in the cubicle next to you. Your team may have several customers. Your customer may be either external (the ultimate consumer of the product or service) or internal (the person or persons to whom you hand off your work).

Figure 1.2. The first fitness area—customer focus.

Often the primary customer is treated with great care and concern while the internal customers are overlooked or treated rudely. Both customers are important to the enterprise.

FITNESS AREA 2: DIRECTION

Definition: Direction defines the unique contribution of the team, from its broadest purposes to its specific actions and activities. Direction shows the fit of the team's and organization's purpose.

Factors: Direction is composed of the following four factors (see Figure 1.3).

1. *Charter*—Formally putting the team into existence.

2. *Vision*—Creating a mental image of what you want your team to contribute in the future.

3. *Mission*—Defining your purpose and your unique contribution to the enterprise.

4. *Goals and objectives*—Broad statements of the desired end results with objectives that spell out the specific actions and activities to obtain those results

How focusing on direction contributes to team fitness

Every team exists for a special purpose. Direction keeps us on target, preventing that age-old mistake, "Ready, fire, aim!" Direction tells us where we are going, specifically what we are trying to achieve, and how we are going to get there. Direction is the mechanism that focuses actions purposefully toward team goals. Clear direction helps set priorities that are essential to assigning resources, and creates commitment and alignment to the team's purpose.

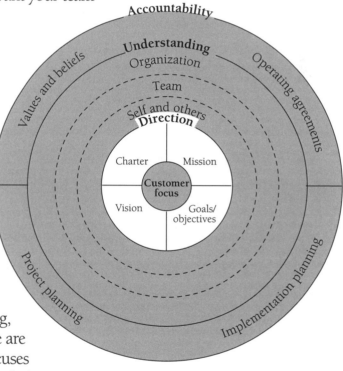

Figure 1.3. The second fitness area—direction.

FITNESS AREA 3: UNDERSTANDING

Definition: Understanding means learning and interpreting the inherent nature of ourselves, our team members, and our organization (see Figure 1.4).

Factors: Areas where the team can improve effectiveness by increasing understanding are

1. *Self and others*—Increasing awareness of and using the strengths and differences in each team member, including yourself.

2. *Teams*—Understanding the dynamics that occur in teamwork approaches to problem solving and decision making.

3. *Organization*—Understanding the norms and culture of the organization and how to get things done in that culture.

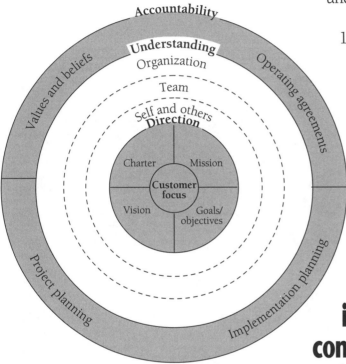

Figure 1.4. The third fitness area—understanding.

How focusing on increasing understanding contributes to team fitness

Team members come to see each other as unique individuals and understand the strength that comes from the diversity of team members. They create a dynamic environment in which the resulting power and synergy helps them see a situation, opportunity, or problem from many different sides. They use team member talents well and they coach and help develop members to be successful. They understand the culture of their organization and how to use the systems and informal political network to achieve team goals.

FITNESS AREA 4: ACCOUNTABILITY

Definition: Accountability is the process of mutually agreeing on what results the team is expected to achieve, specific projects and plans, and how the team will be responsible to the organization and to one another.

Factors: There are four factors that influence the team's accountability (see Figure 1.5).

1. *Values and beliefs*—The beliefs held by the organization and by the team, by which the team is expected to live.

2. *Operating agreements*—The ways team members agree to behave and work together.

3. *Project planning*—The planning methods used to ensure the right things are done, done right, done in the right sequence, and on schedule.

4. *Implementation planning*–The planning methods used to ensure that the project plans and the work of the team will be accepted by the rest of the organization.

How focusing on accountability contributes to team fitness

There are two kinds of accountability for the team to consider—accountability within the team itself, and accountability to those outside the team. Asking "Who does what around here?" helps prevent conflict. Clarifying underlying values and beliefs promotes effective decision making. Planning for implementation ensures action.

Team fitness does not happen by chance. It requires concentrated attention to each of the four areas: customer focus, direction, understanding, and accountability. All teams will have areas of strength and areas that need focus. Your team might need concentrated effort in one of the areas for a time, and then may move to another area, or you could need to work in more than one area at the same time. Part 2 includes an assessment survey that your team can use to zero in on your needs and to get a snapshot of what is already in place and working for you.

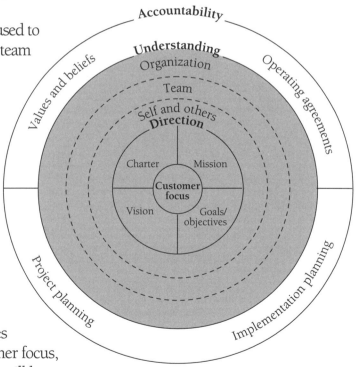

Figure 1.5. The fourth fitness area—accountability.

part two

THE FITNESS METER

Characteristics of Effective Teams

As one examines the teams that seem most fit, several common themes become apparent. How well do the following statements describe your team?

1. They produce results. They capitalize on the strengths of their members to produce extraordinary results, results that individuals working alone cannot do.

2. The purpose of the team is clear and members feel it is worthwhile. They see how they can make a difference. They are more focused on meeting that purpose and satisfying their customers than on their own personal issues or agendas.

3. Members feel invested in the success of the team and accountable for the output of their team.

4. They seem to have fun doing it, even when they are working harder than most other groups. There is an observable spirit and energy.

5. People are clear on their roles. There is no confusion about who does what.

Teams for Global Competition and Speed

The emphasis on swift global competition is driving companies to redo and renew the way things are done on a continuous basis, involving everyone from employees to shareholders. This process stresses teamwork. "The 1990s are proving to be the decade when the soft stuff—like how you listen to employees and customers—finally gets some respect."

J. Solomon, "Fall of the Dinosaurs," *Newsweek,* February 8, 1993, 42–44.

6. Nothing is under the table. Issues and concerns are shared openly, without attack. Issues and concerns are used as a healthy way to surface diverse points of view and generate creative solutions.

7. Team members are not afraid to surface a problem that may impact the entire team's performance. Trust, collaboration, and candid discussion are evident.

8. The team does not lose sight of its goal and become enmeshed in power struggles. Instead, the eye is clearly focused on achieving the team mission and moving toward the vision. This higher purpose transcends the day-to-day ups and downs and makes power politics appear trivial and unimportant.

Often we ask our workshop participants what they believe are the ingredients of the best teams. Some of their responses are

- They have strong, shared values.

- They overcame obstacles and handicaps.

- They incorporate and represent diverse perspectives.

- They are protective and supportive of one another.

- There is a submission of self for the good of the team.

- They share a strong common goal.

The model in Part I and the self report survey in Part II that follows are based on the themes and ingredients discussed herein.

Some of these attributes already exist in your team. Some may need to be developed.

BEGINNER, INTERMEDIATE, AND EXPERT TEAMS

What kind of shape is your team in today? How can you tell what its strengths and need areas are? Like any good fitness program, it is wise to start with a snapshot of your team at present. What is in place already? Where do you need to focus attention now? What is going to be your overall approach?

Snapshot of your team

Team fitness is like skiing. Some teams are experts and can navigate the black diamond runs of their organization. They are in good shape and their skills only need fine tuning. Others may be beginners, just starting up and needing the basics. Some may be intermediates, moving toward the more demanding challenges.

Asking each team member to fill out the fitness meter is the first step. It will help you determine the fitness level of your team and give you an idea of the specific areas where your team needs to work.

THE FITNESS METER

Instructions: To the left of each item is a scale for your response. Take a minute to think about each item and the extent to which it describes your team. Is this statement *true* (T), *more true than false* (MT), *more false than true* (MF), or is it *false* (F)? Check the appropriate box to record your opinion.

Customer focus

T MT MF F

1. Our team has clearly identified the customers who receive our work.

2. Our team has prioritized our customers.

TEAM FITNESS METER

3. We have discussed the customers' expectations for our work.

4. We understand how our customers use our work.

5. We have met with our internal and/or external customers to clarify their expectations for our work.

6. We know how we measure up to our customers' expectations.

How do you measure up?

7. We work in partnership with our customers.

Direction

8. We are clear about what other interested parties, who have a stake in our work, expect from the team.

9. We are clear about the scope and boundaries of our work.

10. Our team has a vision of what we would like to accomplish in the future.

11. Our team's vision inspires us.

12. Our team has an agreed-upon mission.

13. The mission of our team is more important than individual goals.

14. Our individual goals and objectives support the mission and vision of our team.

15. We know how our team will be measured.

16. Our team has specific goals and objectives to which we all are committed.

17. We work together to accomplish our team goals.

Understanding

18. I understand my own strengths and weaknesses—where I make a valuable contribution to the team and where I may need help.

19. I understand the strengths and weaknesses of the other team members—how they contribute to the team, and where they may need help.

20. The climate in our team is one where everyone helps each other when necessary to accomplish the work.

21. Once decisions are made, all team members support them.

22. Team members feel free to bring forward problems that may affect the team's performance.

23. We focus both on getting the work done and how we work together to get it done.

24. Our discussions at team meetings are filled with open participation.

25. We understand our organization and how our team fits into the big picture.

26. We know how to get organizational resources to support our team.

Accountability

27. We have a set of values and beliefs that guide decisions about our work.

28. We have a set of operating agreements about how to work together that team members strive to live up to.

29. We have decided how we will deal with failure to live up to our agreements.

30. We have decided how decisions affecting the whole team will be made.

31. Each team member's role is clear so there is no duplication of effort or things falling through the cracks.

32. We know who is responsible for what, who needs to be informed, and who, if anyone, has veto power.

33. We have prioritized our major goals.

34. We have a project plan that outlines our major milestones and our completion dates.

35. We have identified and analyzed the concerns of our stakeholders, people who have an interest in our work.

36. We have a plan for implementation of the team's work.

Scoring

Give each question the following points.

True	= 8
More true than false	= 6
More false than true	= 4
False	= 2

Compute the average for each item. The mid-point of the range from 2 to 8 is 5.

What's your score?

- Any score over 5 means that the statement is more true than false.

- Any score under 5 means that the statement is more false than true.

A perfect score on any item would be 8. Remember, however, that some people are reluctant to see anything as completely true. They always can remember instances when the situation was different from the desirable outcome.

- An average score of 6 or more demonstrates a team strength.

- An average score under 4 requires study.

- An average score 3 and under is a need area.

In skier jargon: 6 or over is an Expert
3 to 6 is an Intermediate
under 3 is a Beginner

The following score sheet will help you score the fitness meter, once all team members have completed it.

FITNESS METER SCORE SHEET

Scoring: Tally the scores for the responses all team members gave for each item. This will give you the distribution of the process. Using the 8-6-4-2 scales, figure the average for each item.

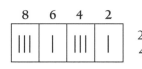

8	6	4	2

24 + 6 + 12 + 2 = **44**
44 (total from above) ÷ **8** (number of team members) = **Avg. 5.5**

Customer focus

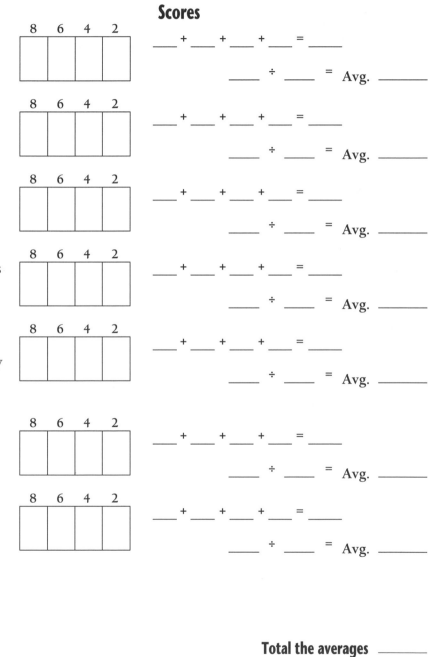

1. Our team has clearly identified the customers who receive our work.

2. Our team has prioritized our customers.

3. We have discussed the customers' expectations for our work.

4. We understand how our customers use our work.

5. We have met with our internal and/or external customers to clarify their expectations for our work.

6. We know how we measure up to our customers' expectations.

7. We work in partnership with our customers.

Scores

___ + ___ + ___ + ___ = ___
___ ÷ ___ = Avg. ___

___ + ___ + ___ + ___ = ___
___ ÷ ___ = Avg. ___

___ + ___ + ___ + ___ = ___
___ ÷ ___ = Avg. ___

___ + ___ + ___ + ___ = ___
___ ÷ ___ = Avg. ___

___ + ___ + ___ + ___ = ___
___ ÷ ___ = Avg. ___

___ + ___ + ___ + ___ = ___
___ ÷ ___ = Avg. ___

___ + ___ + ___ + ___ = ___
___ ÷ ___ = Avg. ___

Total the averages ___

Divide by 7 to get overall customer focus score ___

Direction

Scores

8. We are clear about what other interested parties, who have a stake in our work, expect from the team.

8 6 4 2

___ + ___ + ___ + ___ = ___

___ ÷ ___ = Avg. ___

9. We are clear about the scope and boundaries of our work.

8 6 4 2

___ + ___ + ___ + ___ = ___

___ ÷ ___ = Avg. ___

10. Our team has a vision of what we would like to accomplish in the future.

8 6 4 2

___ + ___ + ___ + ___ = ___

___ ÷ ___ = Avg. ___

11. Our team's vision inspires us.

8 6 4 2

___ + ___ + ___ + ___ = ___

___ ÷ ___ = Avg. ___

12. Our team has an agreed-upon mission.

8 6 4 2

___ + ___ + ___ + ___ = ___

___ ÷ ___ = Avg. ___

13. The mission of our team is more important than individual goals.

8 6 4 2

___ + ___ + ___ + ___ = ___

___ ÷ ___ = Avg. ___

14. Our individual goals and objectives support the mission and vision of our team.

8 6 4 2

___ + ___ + ___ + ___ = ___

___ ÷ ___ = Avg. ___

15. We know how our team will be measured.

8 6 4 2

___ + ___ + ___ + ___ = ___

___ ÷ ___ = Avg. ___

16. Our team has specific goals and objectives to which we all are committed.

8 6 4 2

___ + ___ + ___ + ___ = ___

___ ÷ ___ = Avg. ___

17. We work together to accomplish our team's goals.

8 6 4 2

___ + ___ + ___ + ___ = ___

___ ÷ ___ = Avg. ___

Total the averages ___

Divide by 10 to get overall direction score ___

Understanding

Scores

18. I understand my own strengths and weaknesses—where I make a valuable contribution to the team and where I may need help.

8	6	4	2

___ + ___ + ___ + ___ = ___

___ ÷ ___ = Avg. ___

19. I understand the strengths and weaknesses of the other team members—how they contribute to the team and where they may need help.

8	6	4	2

___ + ___ + ___ + ___ = ___

___ ÷ ___ = Avg. ___

20. The climate in our team is one where everyone helps each other when necessary to accomplish the work.

8	6	4	2

___ + ___ + ___ + ___ = ___

___ ÷ ___ = Avg. ___

21. Once decisions are made, all team members support them.

8	6	4	2

___ + ___ + ___ + ___ = ___

___ ÷ ___ = Avg. ___

22. Team members feel free to bring forward problems that may affect the team's performance.

8	6	4	2

___ + ___ + ___ + ___ = ___

___ ÷ ___ = Avg. ___

23. We focus both on getting the work done and how we work together to get it done.

8	6	4	2

___ + ___ + ___ + ___ = ___

___ ÷ ___ = Avg. ___

24. Our discussions at team meetings are filled with open participation.

8	6	4	2

___ + ___ + ___ + ___ = ___

___ ÷ ___ = Avg. ___

25. We understand our organization and how our team fits into the big picture.

8	6	4	2

___ + ___ + ___ + ___ = ___

___ ÷ ___ = Avg. ___

26. We know how to get organizational resources to support our team.

8	6	4	2

___ + ___ + ___ + ___ = ___

___ ÷ ___ = Avg. ___

Total the averages ___

Divide by 9 to get overall understanding score ___

Accountability

Scores

27. We have a set of values and beliefs that guide decisions about our work.

8 6 4 2

___ + ___ + ___ + ___ = ___

___ ÷ ___ = **Avg.** ___

28. We have a set of operating agreements about how to work together that team members strive to live up to.

8 6 4 2

___ + ___ + ___ + ___ = ___

___ ÷ ___ = **Avg.** ___

29. We have decided how we will deal with failure to live up to our agreements.

8 6 4 2

___ + ___ + ___ + ___ = ___

___ ÷ ___ = **Avg.** ___

30. We have decided how decisions affecting the whole team will be made.

8 6 4 2

___ + ___ + ___ + ___ = ___

___ ÷ ___ = **Avg.** ___

31. Each team member's role is clear so there is no duplication of effort or things falling through the cracks.

8 6 4 2

___ + ___ + ___ + ___ = ___

___ ÷ ___ = **Avg.** ___

32. We know who is responsible for what, who needs to be informed, and who, if anyone, has veto power.

8 6 4 2

___ + ___ + ___ + ___ = ___

___ ÷ ___ = **Avg.** ___

33. We have proioritized our major goals.

8 6 4 2

___ + ___ + ___ + ___ = ___

___ ÷ ___ = **Avg.** ___

34. We have a project plan that outlines major milestones and our completion dates.

8 6 4 2

___ + ___ + ___ + ___ = ___

___ ÷ ___ = **Avg.** ___

35. We have identified and analyzed the concerns of our stakeholders, people who have an interest in our work.

8 6 4 2

___ + ___ + ___ + ___ = ___

___ ÷ ___ = **Avg.** ___

36. We have a plan for implementation of the team's work.

8 6 4 2

___ + ___ + ___ + ___ = ___

___ ÷ ___ = **Avg.** ___

Total the averages ___

Divide by 10 to get overall accountability score ___

TEAM FITNESS ANALYSIS

Team: _____

Date: _____

Instructions: Place an X in the box where your team's average goes. Transfer your scores from the Fitness Meter Score Sheet to complete this analysis.

Our Team Fitness Scores

	Expert 6+	Intermediate 3–6	Beginner 2–3

Customer focus
  Identify
  Clarify expectations			

Direction
  Charter
  Vision
  Mission
  Goals and objectives			

Understanding
  Self and others
  Team
  Organization			

Accountability
  Values and beliefs
  Operating
    agreements
  Project planning
  Implementation
    planning			

The averages can help your team determine areas of need. Within each of the four areas, you can examine your tally marks to determine more specifically where work is needed.

FITNESS PLANNING

You have seen the model of the four areas that contribute to team fitness. You have assessed your strengths and needs in the four areas.

Now it is time to use that information to make a plan and get at it. Use the exercises and explanations that make up the remainder of this workbook to build your team's approach to maximum fitness and to achieve optimum results.

1. *Determine where to start.*

   Select a focus area. Those areas on the fitness model that are closest to the center of the model frequently make good beginning places, such as direction or customer focus. Choose the one(s) that promises the greatest payoff for your team. To ensure success, you may want to look for an area that will boost your team's confidence while furthering its task. The sequence is up to you and your team's needs.

   - Customer focus—Start with the *customer.* Most teams think they know what the customer expects of them and most teams are correct, but only partially correct. Often teams have not actually sat down with their customers, particularly the internal customers, and asked the right questions that define and clarify customer expectations in a nonthreatening way. Fit teams know their customers inside and out. They have made clear agreements with them on what is required and how to meet expectations for working together. They have a strong, active feedback vehicle.

   - Direction—It may be that your team needs to focus on an agreed-upon direction. Do you have a clear purpose and common goal? Does the team have something to drive toward that also helps with day-to-day prioritization of activities? Without direction, team activities for understanding and accountability are frills that have no meaning.

   - Understanding—Did you show a need for accepting differences in team members, or how the team should work together? Read the exercises in the understanding section. When teams are fit in this area, they know how to ensure positive dynamics that support achieving their mission. They know how to influence their leader.

They know how to behave differently in varied situations to achieve results. When all members have this depth of understanding and context for their work, they can operate in any part of the world or on any project independently.

- Accountability—Accountability provides the way to avoid stepping on each others' toes. Members know what they can expect from each other and where to get support. Clear agreements on who does what, on how meetings will run, on follow-through for commitments, are central to the way they operate.

Select the areas that will be most beneficial and fill out the team fitness plan that follows. Developing a systematic approach for the exercises that build your team's fitness in these areas will make your team's work life a healthy, more fulfilling experience.

2. *Plan one team meeting and a follow up. Take one area and start there.* If you are a new team, refer to the new team start-up sequence found in Appendix B. The suggested script example found in Appendix C will be useful for an existing team.

3. *Project ahead what the next step might be and propose it at the end of your first meeting.* Work together with your team to develop a schedule and a fitness plan. Select an exercise from each area in the beginning. The sequence should be adapted to your team's needs identified in the Fitness Meter. Use the Team Fitness Schedule to plan each fitness area and exercise. Set aside specific dates to work on your team's fitness. Begin slowly and work toward fine-tuning and maintenance.

4. *Continue to work and plan ahead on a systematic basis.* Remember, fitness of your body or your team is not built in a day. Regular work over a period of time is the most effective strategy. Good luck!

Team Fitness Schedule

Area	Exercise No.	Date
1.		
2.		
3.		
4.		
5.		
6.		
7.		
8.		
9.		
10.		

part three

THE EXERCISES

Fitness Area I:
Customer Focus Exercises

Definition: Customer focus is getting clear on the expectations, values, and priorities of those who receive the output of your work.

About customer focus

There are two main facets to this process. First, define your particular customer(s) and then find out what is expected of you. In order to be competitive, your customers must perceive that you provide unique value. After you define the customers and their expectations, plan your work in a way that directly helps to achieve this. You can use this same approach to create a better working relationship with your suppliers.

Customer focus actions

Activities for this area include brainstorming, interviews, questionnaires, focus groups, research, and trips to customer locations to see your product or service as it is being used.

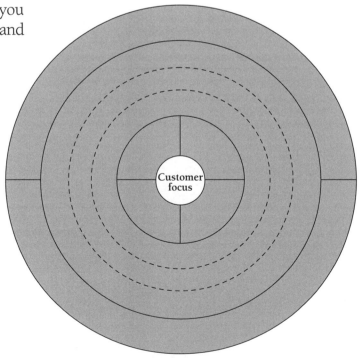

Customer focus questions

- What are the outputs of our work?

- Who receives our outputs?

- What are our customers' expectations for those outputs and the way we work?

- How can we check our assumptions for accuracy directly with our customers?

Exercises in this section

- Customer Focus Factor No. 1: Customer Identification

  1. Who Is the Customer?

  2. Primary Customer Identification

- Customer Focus Factor No. 2: Customer Needs and Expectations

  3. Customer Feedback and Measures

  4. Customer Priorities

  5. What Do Our Customers Want and Expect from Us?

  6. Moments of Truth

  7. Moments of Truth Map

  8. Customer Site Visits

  9. Focus Groups for Internal or External Customers

  10. Surveys

  11. Tracking the Work

  12. Walk a Mile in My Shoes

CUSTOMER FOCUS FACTOR NO. 1
Customer Identification

Definition: The customer is the person who receives your work output, whether it is a product or service.

About customer identification

Customer identification appears to be a very simple process. Most teams can identify the end user or ultimate consumer of their product or services. However, many forget the internal customers, the next person or department that is the receiver of their work. Other customers can be as diverse as regulators, auditors, community members, or boards of directors. Each of these customers must be satisfied for the smooth functioning of the team and organization. Exercises in this section include identifying all possible customers and determining which are primary.

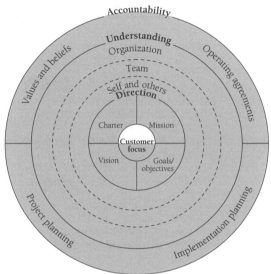

Customer identification questions include

- Who is the customer of your products or service?

- Which of those customers are primary?

- How can we work in partnership with our customers?

CUSTOMER FOCUS EXERCISE NO. 1
Who Is the Customer?

Workout Plan

When to use
As the first step in the customer focus area, it is critical to determine who all the customers are, not just the obvious ones.

Time
30 minutes to 1 hour

Materials
Flip chart paper, masking tape, marking pens

Purpose/objectives

- To identify the primary customers of the team

- To identify some of the less apparent customers for the team

Grouping
All members of the team

Warm-up
Review the purpose for the session. In order to focus on the customer, we must first identify who it is! This is not always as straightforward as it may seem. There always is the customer who is the end user of the organization's products or services. There also are internal customers who receive our work. These may be other people within our team, another department within the company, a regulator or inspector, others in an assembly line. The primary question to ask is "Who are the receivers of our work?"

Aerobics

1. Brainstorm all the possible customers of your team. Every one the team can think of should be listed.

2. Clarify any customers who may be unclear to anyone on the team. Combine any that are listed slightly differently, but are really the same.

3. Group them first under the headings *Internal* and *External*. It may be beneficial to group them into categories such as regulators, auditors, inspectors, and so forth.

Cooldown

Now that we have identified the primary customers of our team, we must think about when and where to focus our activities in addition to what expectations those customers have for our work. Move on to other exercises in this area to help clarify customer needs and wants.

CUSTOMER FOCUS EXERCISE NO. 2
Primary Customer Identificaton

Workout Plan

When to use
After you have identified your customers, you probably will find that you have quite a few. Some customers are primary and others are secondary. Use this exercise to clarify which are your team's primary customers.

Primary customers: Those who receive our work—without whom we would go out of business (internal customers, external customers, end users).

Secondary customers: Those whose concerns also must be considered, but who are not the direct focus of our business (boards, regulators, auditors, steering teams, champions).

Time
30 minutes

Materials
Flip chart, masking tape, marking pens

Purpose/objectives

- To identify your various customers as primary or secondary

Grouping
The entire team

Warm-up
As we go about our daily work, it is important for us to remember which customers should be our focus in scheduling, resources, and time.

Aerobics

List the various customers of the group. Using the worksheet, work together to determine which customers are primary and secondary.

Cooldown

What does this mean to us during times of stress? How do we balance our priorities? What conversations must we have with our customers to help them know what to expect? Having this clear in mind helps teams reprioritize and stay focused on critical, rather than trivial, aspects of their work.

Customer Focus Worksheet—Exercise No. 2
Determining Primary Customers

1. List customers, both internal and external.

2. Rearrange the customer list into primary and secondary customers, in order, top to bottom.

3. Develop hypothetical cases where there are conflicting demands on the team from various customers. Answer the question, "How do we best handle this situation?"

Order   **Customers**

_____   • _____

_____   • _____

_____   • _____

_____   • _____

_____   • _____

_____   • _____

_____   • _____

_____   • _____

_____   • _____

_____   • _____

CUSTOMER FOCUS FACTOR NO. 2
Customer Needs and Expectations

Definition: Getting clear on the expectations, needs, wants, and priorities of those who receive your work.

About customer needs and expectations

Customer expectations go beyond the product or service you provide. Positive customer relationships and loyalty often are based on the ease of doing business with you—how billing is done, how messages are delivered, or how problems are handled. The feelings of trust and confidence, or lack of it, that result from these additional factors make or break many customer relationships over time.

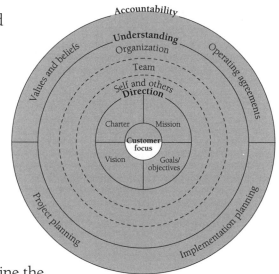

Organizations often have extensive means in place to determine the needs and expectations of the end user, but not of the internal customer—the person within the organization to whom your team delivers its work.

Customer needs and expectations actions

Talking face to face with the customer, whether in interviews, focus groups, or site visits, is effective in understanding needs and priorities. The team may first discuss what it believes the customer's expectations are and then follow through by directly checking its assumptions with the customer.

What do customers expect?

Customer needs and expectations questions

- What are the customers' requirements for what we provide?

- What are the wants and expectations our customers have for doing business with us?

- What would delight our customers?

- When push comes to shove, what is most important to our customers?

- How can we check the accuracy of our assumptions directly with our customers?

CUSTOMER FOCUS EXERCISE NO. 3
Customer Feedback and Measures

Workout Plan

When to use
Shortly after a new customer relationship has been put in place, or at any time as customer priorities are established or reestablished.

Time
2 to 3 hours

Materials
Flip chart, markers

Purpose/objectives

- To identify customer expectations

- Inventory present methods for customer feedback and our measures for meeting customer needs

Grouping
All team members

Warm-up
Clarify the focus of activities to be analyzed. Is it one area of work (providing activity report)? Is it a group of processes or work activities (leadership development)? Is it the work of a team? Try to keep the focus as small as possible.

Aerobics

1. Brainstorm all possible customers for the work output(s) involved. Who receives our work?

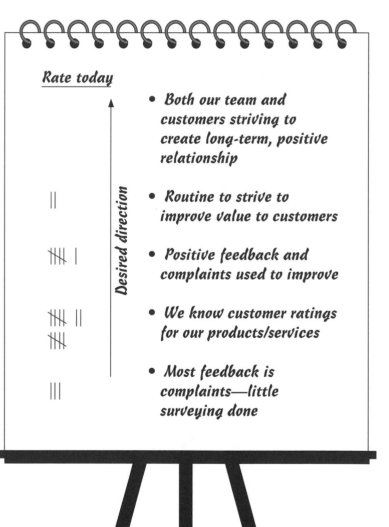

Rate today

Desired direction

- **Both our team and customers striving to create long-term, positive relationship**

- **Routine to strive to improve value to customers**

- **Positive feedback and complaints used to improve**

- **We know customer ratings for our products/services**

- **Most feedback is complaints—little surveying done**

How is our customer satisfaction?

2. List customers in order from the most primary to the least for that particular work.

3. For each customer, brainstorm what the team sees as the customers' expectations (*what* they require or *how* they want what we deliver and *how* they want us to work with them). Put each list in order from top priority to least priority, according to your team's perceptions of what each customer would say.

4. Develop one list of top customer priorities. (If we could only meet a few, which are most critical? When push comes to shove, what are their highest priorities?)

5. For each item on the primary customer priority list, check to see what measures or feedback mechanisms are in place to help the team know where they stand in the customers' eyes. Are there feedback mechanisms or controls early in the process as well as at the end, so things can be corrected or prevented before the products or services reach the customer?

6. For key areas where there are no present checks or measures, determine a method of ensuring frequent feedback of customer satisfaction for that priority.

Cooldown
Find a way to validate the team's thinking with each of the primary customers identified. Can we make a site visit? Could we hold a meeting where we repeat this process with their involvement? What data do we already collect from them? Teams can collect a few vital measures that are targeted to letting them know how they stand on a continuous basis.

CUSTOMER FOCUS EXERCISE NO. 4
Customer Priorities

Workout Plan

When to use
When there is a need to clarify where to put time and energy. This is a way to use research to help clarify customer needs and wants.

Time
1 hour

Materials
Customer priorities worksheet

Purpose/objectives

- Develop understanding of the requirements, needs, and wants of a customer that go beyond the product or service itself.

- Spell out specifically what customers want in each of 10 categories from research on customer priorities.

- Prioritize what you think is most to least important of the 10 categories for customers.

Grouping
Small groups of two to five who share similar responsibilities

Warm-up
Introduce the idea of ease of doing business with you and the critical factors, in addition to the service or product you provide. Share the ten dimensions of service quality that were identified in the Texas A & M research in 1985.* This research project identified 10 categories that covered the needs and wants of customers, including the specifics for the products and services provided, but also the things in addition to the service or product (Figure 3.1). These categories are included on the worksheet for this exercise.

---

*Leonard L. Berry, Valerie A. Zeithami, and A. Parasuraman, "Quality Counts in Services, Too," *Business Horizons,* May–June 1985, 44–52.

Aerobics

1. In small groups, each group writes examples of what each category looks like for its customer. (In other words, in a technical document publications department *reliability* may mean meeting the company standards; in a hotel it may mean that wake-up calls come within 1 or 2 minutes of the time they were requested; in word processing it may mean accuracy.)

2. After the categories are defined, each group ranks in order which category their customer would give highest priority, next highest, and so on, all the way to the lowest priority.

Cooldown

Debrief—Ask groups to share the surprises they had or the differences in opinion expressed by one group member to another. How does this analysis affect their thinking about how things are presently done? Are there obvious improvements or changes that should be made?

NOTE

The best value from this exercise comes when groups can repeat the same process in a face-to-face meeting with their customers. The discussion of priorities and verifying our perceptions of what is important to our customers can create important changes in emphasis and establishment of work priorities.

Ten dimensions of service quality

Ranking
of importance

___4___   *Reliability:* Consistency of performance
           Looks like—*meet standards/accuracy*

___3___   *Responsiveness:* Timely, readiness to provide service
           Looks like—*flexibility/adequate staffing/reasonable dates*

___1___   *Competence:* Required skills to do it right the first time
           Looks like—*expertise/training/technology*

___5___   *Access:* Approachability and ease of contact
           Looks like—*availability/attitude*

___8___   *Courtesy:* Politeness and respect, clean appearance
           Looks like—*respect our ideas/manners*

___9___   *Communication:* Listening, sharing information, keeping in touch
           Looks like—*listen, not just hear/negotiate*

___7___   *Credibility:* Believability; delivering as promised
           Looks like—*past performance/confidence level*

___10___   *Security:* Freedom from risk
           Looks like—*discretion/confidentiality/professionalism*

___2___   *Understanding:* Clarifying requirements and needs, giving individual attention
           Looks like—*getting to know/figuring out real needs*

___6___   *Tangibles:* Physical evidence of service; tools, personnel, facilities, letters, bills
           Looks like—*products/services/us*

From: Leonard L. Berry, Valerie A. Zeithami, and A. Parasuraman, "Quality Counts in Services, Too," *Business Horizons,* May–June 1985, 44–52.

Example using the ten dimensions of service quality.

Customer Focus Worksheet—Exercise No. 4
Customer Priorities

First define what your customer wants in each area for your particular job. Then rank in order 1 to 10 as the most important to the least important in the eyes of your customer.

Ten dimensions of service quality

Ranking

____ *Reliability:* Consistency of performance

Looks like—
(Example: in a technical document publications department *reliability* may mean meeting the company standards; in a repro department it may mean print quality is consistent; in word processing it may mean accuracy. For your team it may be delivering what was promised on time, or….)

____ *Responsiveness:* Timely, readiness to provide service

Looks like—

____ *Competence:* Required skills to do it right the first time

Looks like—

___ *Access:* Approachability and ease of contact

Looks like—

___ *Courtesy:* Politeness and respect, clean appearance

Looks like—

___ *Communication:* Listening, sharing information, keeping in touch

Looks like—

___ *Credibility:* Believability; delivering as promised

Looks like—

___ *Security:* Freedom from risk

Looks like—

___ *Understanding:* Clarifying requirements and needs, giving individual attention

Looks like—

___ *Tangibles:* Physical evidence of service; tools, personnel, facilities, letters, bills

Looks like—

CUSTOMER FOCUS EXERCISE NO. 5
What Do Our Customers Want and Expect from Us?

Workout Plan

CUSTOMER	EXPECTATIONS
Borrowers	• *Competitive rates* • *Fast, friendly service* • *Products meet needs* • *Easy access to loan officers* • *Special treatment* • *Competent employees to wait on them* • *Loan officers available during off hours*
Examiners	• *Everything complete and in its place* • *Accuracy* • *Sound judgment* • *Use of memos/reports as training tools*
Internal customers	• *Treatment on equal level as we would treat external customers*

How is our customer satisfaction?

When to use
After the team has identified the customers who receive the team's work, this exercise can help clarify the expectations of the various customers. This is an interactive way to explore customer needs and wants.

Time
30 minutes

Materials
Flip chart paper, masking tape, marking pens, results of any market research that has been done

Purpose/objectives

• To clarify the expectations of the team's customers

Grouping
All members of the team.

Warm-up
In order to deliver superior products and services, we need to clarify the expectations of the various customers of our team.

Aerobics

Brainstorm by walking around.

1. List the customers of the team on separate sheets of flip chart paper.

2. Hang the flip charts on the wall.

3. Ask the team members to walk around and make notes on the paper with marking pens on what they think each of the various customers expects from the team. (This may be timeliness, accuracy, error-free billings, zero defects, reliability, and so forth.)

4. After all the ideas have been listed, discuss each set of customers separately.

   - Ask for elaboration of each idea.

   - Try to be as specific as possible (in other words, timeliness; does that mean 30 minutes, 30 days?)

   - Of these expectations, which do you think is most important to the customer?

   - Rank order the customer expectations.

Cooldown

   - How can we check the accuracy of these expectations and priorities by asking our customers directly, through focus groups or questionnaires?

   - If we believe this about our customers' expectations, how will that impact our work?

   - What must we continue to do?

   - What must we start doing?

   - What should we stop doing?

Be sure to record the customer expectations and the cooldown question responses for distribution to all team members.

CUSTOMER FOCUS EXERCISE NO. 6
Moments of Truth

Workout Plan

Customer Needs

"John Longstreet, manager of the Harvey Hotel in Plano, Texas, employs what he calls the 'lobby lizard' approach: Each day a member of his management team (including himself) is in the lobby from 7–9 A.M. to interview departing guests about ways the hotel could improve. One of the team drives the courtesy van to the airport with the same purpose."

C. Bell, "Turning Customers into Partners," *At Work,* March/April 1993, 19.

When to use
As a way to understand and improve the customers' experience as they interact with our team. This exercise focuses on the interface as a critical factor in the customer–supplier relationship.*

Time
1 hour

Materials
Flip chart, colored markers, moments of truth planning worksheet

Purpose/objectives

- Identify the critical interactions with the customer that can either make or break the relationship.

- Build a plan to anticipate what will happen to customers in those interactions.

- Put into place a system for ensuring that critical customer interactions go well.

Grouping
Entire group or in subgroups according to customer interactions

Warm-up
Get the team thinking about moments of truth by looking at the analogy of taking a trip on an airline. Brainstorm moments of truth for a typical trip (checking in, boarding the plane, takeoff, finding your seat, food service, landing, claiming your luggage).

*The Moments of Truth concept originated with Jan Carlzon of Scandinavian Airlines. J. Carlzon, *Moments of Truth* (New York: Harper and Row, 1987).

Aerobics

1. Shift to the team's customers and brainstorm the moments of truth for the customers during their interactions with the team.

2. Determine which of the brainstormed list of moments of truth are most critical in the customers' eyes (in the airline example it probably is takeoff and landing!) The team should come to consensus on the items that are most critical, perhaps a total of four to six.

3. For each of the critical moments identified, use the worksheet to build a proactive plan that ensures that each moment is handled appropriately, so problems are prevented as much as possible, and so if something does go wrong, the team knows exactly how to handle it for minimum negative impact.

Cooldown

Best value and results can be achieved when this process is conducted interactively with the customer face-to-face, or the results of the team's analysis can be presented to the customer for discussion and validation. If this is not possible, some check of the team's perceptions of customer priority is still important.

Customer Focus Worksheet—Exercise No. 6
Moments of Truth Action Plan

Use this planning worksheet to focus on customer expectations and each person's impact on forming a positive relationship.

1. Moment of truth to be managed: _____
   _____
   _____
   _____
   _____

2. The customer's expectation of us: _____
   _____
   _____
   _____
   _____

3. Our plan to meet the expectation: _____
   _____
   _____
   _____
   _____

   a. What we can do immediately: _____
      _____
      _____

   b. What will need some work: _____
      _____
      _____

CUSTOMER FOCUS EXERCISE NO. 7
Moments of Truth Map

Workout Plan

When to use
This exercise is most applicable with a team or company that deals directly with external customers in person or by telephone. The factors used here apply best to service enterprises, and represent those categories from the Texas A & M research by Leonard Berry, David Bennett, and Carter Brown found to apply most specifically to the service industry.*

Time
2 hours

Materials
Moments of truth worksheet, excellence in service quality definitions, flip chart paper, masking tape, marking pens

Purpose/objectives

- To clarify the kinds of treatment the customer receives from your company at all levels

- To improve the service provided in several critical areas

Grouping
All team members. If it is a large group, you may divide into groups of four to six members each.

Warm-up
Jan Carlzon, president of Scandinavian Airlines (SAS) coined the term, *moments of truth*. He uses the term to describe the quality of the contact between the customer and the employees of the firm, usually frontline employees.

*L. L. Berry, D. R. Bennett, and C. W. Brown, *Service Quality: Profit Strategy for Financial Institutions* (Homewood, Ill.: Dow Jones-Irwin, 1989).

Aerobics

1. Assign groups of people to map the moments of truth of typical interactions between customers and the firm's products and employees.

   If the group is small, you may want to map only one of the following areas at a session.

   Areas to consider include

   a. The customer comes to your office or store.
   How easy is it to find?
   How easy is it to park?
   What does the parking lot look like?
   What does the front door look like?
   How is the customer greeted?
   What is the first thing the customer sees?
   What does the waiting room look like?

   b. The customer receives a bill.

   c. The customer calls for information.

   d. The customer calls for an appointment.

   e. The customer calls with a complaint.

   f. Other areas peculiar to your business where the company and the customer have contact.

2. After you have mapped the moments of truth, rate yourself on the scale of service excellence: reliability, responsiveness, assurance, empathy, and tangibles. (Not every quality will apply to every interaction.)

3. Have groups report their findings and discuss them.

4. Choose an area to improve and plan for corrective action. (If you are just starting to look for continuous improvement, choose something that is easy to correct and will give you a quick win.)

Cooldown

Ask the group if there are other interactions between the customer and the company that should be mapped. Ask, "What shall we do to follow up with our maps?" "Are there other people who should be involved in this process who are not here?" Determine several key action items or areas to study for improvements as the outcome of this work.

Customer Focus Worksheet—Exercise No. 7
Excellence in service quality

Reliability. Doing what you said you would do, dependability, accuracy, zero defects. Doing it right the first time.

Looks like: _____

Responsiveness. Readiness to serve, willingness to serve customers promptly and efficiently, ability and willingness to adapt to changing customer requirements.

Looks like:_____

Assurance. Courtesy and competence of service personnel that instill trust and confidence in the customer.

Looks like:_____

_____

Empathy. Commitment to the customer—willingness to understand the customer's point of view and precise needs, and find just the right answer.

Looks like: _____

_____

Tangibles. Visible part of the service—facilities, equipment, brochures, letters, bills, appearance of the contact person.

Looks like:_____

_____

TEAM	A	B	C	
RELIABILITY	2	3	4	
RESPONSIVENESS	4	2	5	
EMPATHY	5	1	2	
ASSURANCE	4	3	1	
TANGIBLES	3			

Service quality counts.

Customer Focus Worksheet—Exercise No. 7
How Do We Rate?

Rate 1 (low)–10 (high) or N/A

Moments of truth	Reliability	Responsiveness	Assurance	Empathy	Tangibles
1.					
2.					
3.					
4.					
5.					
6.					
7.					
8.					
9.					
10.					
11.					
12.					
13.					
14.					
15.					
16.					

CUSTOMER FOCUS EXERCISE NO. 8
Customer Site Visits

Workout Plan

When to use
To see and talk with your customers in their environment in order to understand their expectations in a way that helps you improve the product or service you provide for them.

Time
1 hour to plan for the visit; all day or several days for site visits; one-half day to debrief

Materials
Protocols for site visits sheet, small notebooks for note taking at the site

Purpose/objectives
To get to know your customers better and how they use your product or service

Grouping
The entire team

Warm-up
Planning for the visit ahead is critical to success on the day of the visit.

Study the customers in their environment.

Aerobics

1. Determine the objectives of the visit.

   • To see how the customers use the product or service

   • To get to know the customers better and show concern for their problems

   • To determine if there are ways to improve on the product or service to better serve the customers' needs

2. Determine the specific people necessary to contact at the customer site, plus possible needed approvals in your own organization.

3. Set dates with the site that are convenient for the team and minimize disruption at the site to be visited.

4. Determine how the team should be divided so that there will be several unique experiences to discuss upon return.

5. Go over some of the suggested protocols for site visits and decide what questions should be asked.

6. Plan the logistics for arrival and departure at the site.

7. Pass out information sheet on customer site for everyone to study. This should include company size, locations, revenue, employees, business trends; areas for which they are proud or known, recent achievements.

Ask what questions and concerns people may have about preparing for the site visit.

Cooldown

After the site visit, meet during the same day or the next morning to share your experience with each other. Send a follow-up report of your visit to the sponsors.

CUSTOMER FOCUS INFORMATION SHEET— EXERCISE NO. 8

Protocol for site visits

1. Be sure to explain to the customer site management and employees the purpose of your visit.

2. Look at the activities and results you see; ask why and how questions.

3. Compliment when there is an opportunity.

4. Encourage comments about your products and service—both positive and negative.

5. Take notes. Collect brochures and take pictures (if that is acceptable) to help the rest of the team at home get a true understanding of the customer.

6. Strive for an informal tone, but be professional.

7. Talk to them about their products, service, and customers. See how what you provide links to their ultimate customer. Find out what they consider as their competitive advantage and their major competitors.

8. Take time to tell your hosts what you have learned and how appreciative you are of their time.

Customer Focus Worksheet—Exercise No. 8
Sample site visit interview questions

1. Tell me about the work of your group, department, company.

_____

_____

2. Who are your main customers? Who are their customers?

_____

_____

3. How do you use our products/services?

_____

_____

4. How does what we provide reach the end-user customer?

_____

_____

5. What do you see as your competitive advantage? How does what we do support your advantage?

_____

_____

6. What happens to you if there is a problem with our product or service?

_____

_____

7. What could we do to improve our product/service to make it better for you? For your customers?

_____

_____

8. What advice could you give our department, group, company?

_____

_____

9. Other comments.

_____

_____

Customer Focus Worksheet—Exercise No. 8
Site visit summary

Site visited: _____ Date: _____

Team members: _____
_____
_____

Overall impressions: _____
_____
_____
_____
_____

Key observations: _____
_____
_____
_____
_____

Implications for our team: _____
_____
_____
_____
_____

Action items: _____
_____
_____
_____
_____

CUSTOMER FOCUS EXERCISE NO. 9
Focus Groups for Internal or External Customers

Workout Plan

When to use
When you want to learn directly from your customers about their needs and requirements and how you are doing in meeting them. This meeting also may give you ideas for new products or delivery systems.

Time
1 hour

Materials
Customer focus interview worksheet

Purpose/objectives

- To meet face-to-face with your customers, either internal or external, to define their needs and expectations

- To allow customers to rate your performance against those needs and expectations

Grouping
One to six customers plus at least two members of the team

Warm-up
Tell the customers that you want to find out as much as you can about their current and future needs and expectations. Ask for about one hour of their time to help you determine their requirements and evaluate your performance against those requirements. Mention that you are looking for ways to improve the way you meet their needs.

Aerobics
Ask the customer the questions on the customer focus interview worksheet. One team member asks the questions as another records the responses. Do not use this opportunity to explain or defend anything that is raised. Record their perceptions, even when they are different from your own.

Cooldown

Thank the customers for their help and input. Agree to make changes that are easy to do. Tell them you will study other issues that surfaced. Offer your assistance to them.

Summarize the data you received. Add this information to other focus group interviews and distribute to all team members and other interested parties. This information can become a baseline for team improvement projects. Follow up with customers to let them know how their input was used.

CUSTOMER FOCUS WORKSHEET—EXERCISE NO. 9
Interview format for internal customers

Here are suggestions for interviewers. This format may be used one-on-one, but is preferable with a group of four to six members of the internal customer group. There should be two people from the supplier group, one to question and one to write notes. As you write notes, try to capture exact words and phrases of the people being interviewed without stopping the flow of dialogue.

For the interviewer, this is a time to listen. The perceptions of the customer group may be different from your own perceptions, but don't explain or try to change their perception. Simply listen and record.

Be sure to thank them for their time and information. Let them know they have been heard and that you will use the information they have given you to improve your products and service to them.

Questions

1. Tell me about the work of your group. What are your primary responsibilities and work outputs?

2. What is the importance of the products and services we supply to you?

   To your customers?

3. How would you describe the work of our group?

4. Describe the products (or services) we provide to you.

5. Are there other products or services we could or should provide to you?

6. What are your (needs), (expectations), (requirements) from our group?

7. Please rank your responses to the preceding question in order from most important to least important, with 1 equalling the highest priority.

8. How do we perform on those needs and expectations? (Be as specific as possible.)

a. Where are we strong?

b. Where do we need to improve?

9. If you could choose only one area for us to improve, what would it be and why?

Overall, how would you rate us on the quality of our products and services?

a. Product quality

1	5	10
Poor	Average	Outstanding

b. Service quality

1	5	10
Poor	Average	Outstanding

Customer Focus Worksheet—Exercise No. 9
Interview format for external customers

Suggestions for interviewers. This format may be used one-on-one, but is preferable with a group of four to six members of the firm's customers or potential customers. There should be two people from the firm, one to question and one to write notes. As you write notes, try to capture exact words and phrases of the people being interviewed without stopping the flow of dialogue.

For the interviewer, this is a time to listen. The perceptions of the customer group may be different from your own, but don't try to explain or to change their perceptions. Simply listen and record.

Be sure to thank them for their time and information. Let them know they have been heard and that you will use the information they have given you to improve your products and service to them.

Questions

1. Tell me about your work.

_____
_____
_____
_____

2. What is the importance of the products and services we supply to you?

_____
_____
_____
_____

What is the importance of the products and services we supply to your customers?

_____
_____
_____
_____

3. How would you describe the work of our company?

_____
_____
_____
_____

4. Describe the products we provide to you.

_____
_____
_____
_____

Describe the services we provide to you.

_____
_____
_____
_____

5. Are there other products or services we could or should provide to you?

_____
_____
_____
_____

6. What are your (needs), (expectations), (requirements) from our firm?

_____
_____
_____
_____

7. Please rank your responses to the preceding question in order from most important to least important, with 1 equalling the highest priority.

_____
_____
_____
_____

8. How do we perform on those needs and expectations? (Be as specific as possible.)

_____
_____
_____
_____

a. Where are we strong?

_____
_____
_____
_____

b. Where do we need to improve?

_____

_____

_____

_____

9. Who are our major competitors?

_____

_____

_____

_____

10. How well do they do on the above?

_____

_____

_____

_____

11. If you choose to leave us for our competitor, or work with us instead of the competitor, what would be the primary reason?

_____

_____

_____

_____

12. If you could choose only one area for us to improve, what would it be and why?

_____

_____

_____

_____

Overall, how would you rate us on the quality of our products and services?

a. Product quality

|⎯⎯⎯⎯⎯⎯⎯⎯⎯⎯|⎯⎯⎯⎯⎯⎯⎯⎯⎯⎯|

1   5   10

Poor   Average   Outstanding

b. Service quality

|⎯⎯⎯⎯⎯⎯⎯⎯⎯⎯|⎯⎯⎯⎯⎯⎯⎯⎯⎯⎯|

1   5   10

Poor   Average   Outstanding

CUSTOMER FOCUS EXERCISE NO. 10
Surveys

Workout Plan

When to use
Every team and every company needs feedback on its work. One of the most common and simple ways to get this feedback is with a survey, either on paper or by telephone.

A survey should be simple, short, and easy to answer. Asking people to rate you from 1–10 or 1–5 gives you baseline data that are useful later in checking your progress. Always allow space or time for comments. Surveys are most candid when they are anonymous, or when the person who conducts the survey is impartial.

Time
One hour

Materials
Pencil and paper, flip chart, marking pens, survey worksheets as examples to use when building your own survey

Purpose/objectives

- To develop a survey that will give the team feedback on their work

- To determine whom to survey

- To plan for administering and scoring the survey

Grouping
All team members or a committee of team members

Warm-up
Remind the team that feedback will help them to improve and will uncover subtle problems or complaints their customers may have about their products and services.

Aerobics

1. Generate ideas for questions. Good sources for questions can be focus group information or critical incidents, both positive and negative. Remember to consider questions about your product or service, and the delivery of your product or service.

2. Group the ideas into categories.

3. Write a short, declarative statement that describes your product or service. Be sure to include only one idea per sentence. You may have several ideas under one category.

4. The categories can become dimensions. For example, under *Reliability* as a dimension, you might have one to three items.

   • "Delivers what they say they will on time every time."

   • "Delivers their product to us without defects."

   • "Calls us as soon as possible, if there is a snag in delivery date."

5. Develop a rating scale for each item.

6. To keep your survey short, use only a few items from the item pool under each dimension on a particular survey.

Cooldown

Plan now to pilot your survey on people outside your team to test for clarity of the questions, to catch any jargon, to determine if you are asking the questions that are most important to your customers. Meet again to discuss the results of your pilot and make plans to survey your target population.

NOTE
How will you use the results of your survey?

- You can analyze the gap between the current and the ideal.

- You can use it as baseline data for performance measurement.

- You can use the results to determine priorities for resources.

- The results may show you where you need more training.

- The results can pinpoint areas where your processes may be ineffective.

CUSTOMER FOCUS INFORMATION SHEET—EXERCISE NO. 10

Sample survey for a service firm

Please circle the appropriate number for each question and make any specific comments regarding our performance.

1. How consistent is our performance?

   1   2   3   4   5
   Poor   Excellent

2. How well do we honor our promises?

   1   2   3   4   5
   Poor   Excellent

3. How responsive have we been to your time requirements?

   1   2   3   4   5
   Poor   Excellent

4. How knowledgeable/competent do you believe we are in our field?

   1   2   3   4   5
   Poor   Excellent

5. How easy are we to contact?

   1   2   3   4   5
   Poor   Excellent

6. How responsive are we in getting back to you when you leave a message?

   1   2   3   4   5
   Poor   Excellent

7. Are we courteous and polite?

   1   2   3   4   5
   Poor   Excellent

8. Do we treat you with respect?

   1   2   3   4   5
   Poor   Excellent

9. Is the information you get from us clear and concise?

   1   2   3   4   5
   Poor   Excellent

10. How well do we listen to you?

   1   2   3   4   5
   Poor   Excellent

11. Do you believe that we have your best interests at heart?

   1   2   3   4   5
   Poor   Excellent

12. How well do we tailor our work to your specific needs and requirements?

1   2   3   4   5
Poor   Excellent

13. Do you feel we really understand your needs?

1   2   3   4   5
Poor   Excellent

14. How effective are we overall in helping you achieve your goals?

1   2   3   4   5
Poor   Excellent

15. What advice can you give us to help us provide even better service?

CUSTOMER FOCUS EXERCISE NO. 11
Tracking the Work

Workout Plan

When to use
This exercise is most effective in a large organization where the next department is the team's customer. It is particularly useful when there are several handoffs in administrative areas, or when the work is sequential from person to person.

Time
Varies with the number of people and complexity of the interactions; approximately one-half day, with a scheduled follow-up

Smooth handoffs ease the flow.

Materials
Copies of work products, flip chart, masking tape, marking pens

Purpose/objectives

- To understand the flow of work between departments

- To understand the next department's needs and requirements for the team's work, and your needs and requirements from them

- To clarify expectations and timelines

Grouping
All members of each department who have interaction with each other

Warm-up
The two department leaders open the meeting, offering some appropriate remarks; for example, "Sometimes we have conflict and crisis between our departments. We want to work together, but as we get caught up in our jobs and deadlines, we forget about the needs of our internal customers. Today we are going to track the flow of our work between the two departments and get clear on what is needed and what kinds of deadlines are required."

Aerobics

1. Ask people to arrange themselves as the work might flow. The first person who receives the work answers the following questions:

   • Where does the work come from? (Another department, the telephone, the fax?)

   • What do I do to it?

   • Where do I put it?

   • What must be included to be complete and accurate?

   • What are my deadlines for completion? Leaders draw a flowchart on the flip chart. Put answers to the questions on Post-it® notes and stick to the flowchart as it grows.

2. This person passes the work to the next person who receives it. That second person answers the same questions.

3. This process continues until the whole process is diagrammed on the flowchart.

4. Then ask the following questions:

   • Where are the glitches?

   • What could we do to help you?

   • What can you do to help us?

   • Are there other people who could help us both? Who needs to be involved?

   • What can we learn from being both customers and suppliers to each other?

   • Are there ways to simplify the flow?

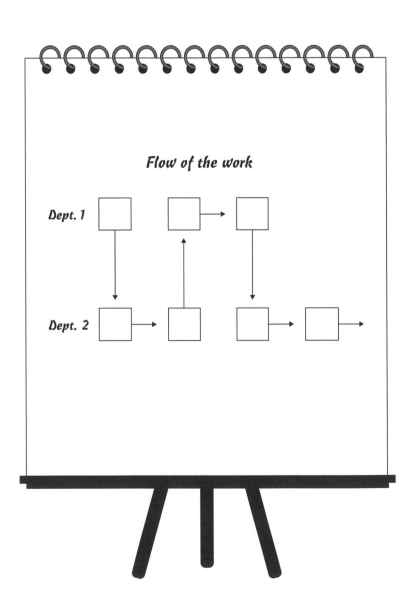

Flow of the work

Dept. 1

Dept. 2

5. Problem solve the issues.

6. Make plans for improvement.

7. Schedule a follow-up meeting to see how the plans are working.

Cooldown
Summarize the progress that has been made at this session. Review the action plans, timetables, and responsibilities. Ask for each person's reactions to the exercise. Are there other areas where this exercise would be useful?

Thank the other department team members for their help. Assure them of your team's support.

CUSTOMER FOCUS EXERCISE NO. 12
Walk a Mile in My Shoes

Workout Plan

When to use
Use this exercise to identify customer expectations and complaints, and dramatize how we may be perceived by the customer. This is a good exercise to use to get rid of tensions in a customer–supplier relationship and to build a way of working together to create a stronger partnership.

Time
30 minutes to 1 hour.

Materials
Table (preferably round) with four to six chairs, flip chart paper, masking tape, marking pens

Purpose/objectives

- To clarify how the team is currently seen by its customers and define how the team prefers to be seen

- To plan for corrective action to improve customer perceptions

Grouping
All team members

Warm-up
Select the names of four to six of your primary customers. They may be internal customers or external end users of your products and/or services. Ask team members to volunteer to play the role of one of the customers until you have a team member for each identified customer. Team members not playing a role can coach those who are.

Aerobics

1. Ask the role players to sit as customers around the table. Ask the role players to describe their experiences with the team, carrying on a conversation with the other role players about what it is like to do

business with you. Descriptions should include positive and negative experiences. Allow 15 minutes minimum for this conversation.

2. After the conversation is finished, ask all team members these questions.

   • What pleased you?

   • What surprised you?

   • What do you wish were different?

3. Record the responses on flip chart paper.

4. Action planning.

   • Where can we build on our strengths?

   • Where do we need to improve?

   • What should we do about it?

Cooldown

Record the areas for improvement and the plans developed. Be sure these are distributed to every team member and other interested stakeholders. Schedule a follow-up meeting to check on progress against the plans.

Fitness Area II: Direction Exercises

Definition: Direction defines the unique contribution of the team, from its broadest purposes to its specific actions and activities.

About direction

Clear direction is at the heart of an effective team. It is necessary to focus the team's actions to reliably meet the customers' expectations and to drive toward the team's vision and mission. Without direction, other team development activities can be superfluous.

Teams who have clear direction understand their vision, have a well-defined mission, have specific goals and objectives, are clear about their boundaries and know what is expected of them. This clarity ensures all team member actions are aligned and driving toward the common purpose of the team.

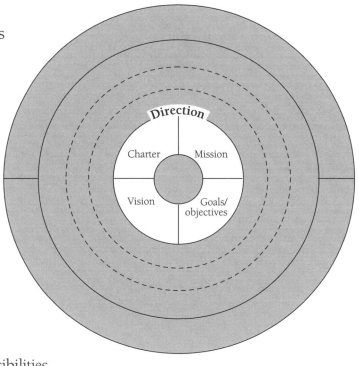

Direction actions

Meetings with the team's sponsor to spell out responsibilities and accountabilities followed by team work on vision, mission, and goals help get all members on the same wavelength.

Leasing Company Vision, Mission, Goals

Vision

_____ Leasing company will be the recognized leader in leasing and related financial services in the United States.

This means we will be known to our public for

1. Effective products (needed, value, profitable, competitive)

2. Customer responsiveness (call them—they'll get it done!)

3. Aggressive growth (fastest growing in our market niche)

Mission

_____ Leasing company will

Provide competitive leasing and innovative financial services beneficial to its customers and stockholders.

Preserve and enhance its financial stability through profit-oriented marketing practices, efficient administrative operations, and orderly growth.

Goals

1. Generate returns equal to or better than our respected competitors.

2. Obtain 2 percent of capital financing by year end and 4 percent in five years.

3. Develop significant vendor financing relationships.

4. Be fully supported and respected by our public.

5. Be a dynamic and innovative organization.

Sample vision, mission, and goals for a leasing company.

Direction questions

- What is our unique contribution to the organization?

- What would it look like if we were contributing what we would most like to contribute in the organization?

- What are the boundaries and givens within which we work?

- Are the goals and objectives of individuals aligned with those of the team and organization?

Exercises in this section

- Direction Factor No. 1: Charter

  1. Project of Task Team New Team Charter

  2. Long-Term or Ongoing Team Chartering Meeting

- Direction Factor No. 2: Vision

  3. A One-Day Visioning Meeting

  4. Warm-Up Vision

  5. Creating a Team Vision—with Pictures

- Direction Factor No. 3: Mission

  6. Mission Statement

  7. Short Mission Statement

- Direction Factor No. 4: Goals and Objectives

  8. Goals and Objectives—Top Down

  9. Bottom-Up Goal Setting

  10. Which Goals Have Priority?

DIRECTION FACTOR NO. 1
Charter

Definition: Chartering of the team means formally putting the team into existence with a clear scope and expectations.

Do we have the necessary resources?

About chartering

A team is formed to meet some purpose for the organization. In the chartering process, the team and whoever is sponsoring or accountable for them meet face-to-face to establish clear expectations and boundaries for the team's work. Teams that have been in existence for a while also may need to clarify charter expectations if that was not done initially, or if the direction of the organization has created the need for changes.

Chartering actions

Best clarity and team member commitment can be achieved if the chartering process takes place with all team members and the sponsor meeting together, so that all questions and clarification can be made person-to-person.

Chartering questions

- What processes is this team responsible for and why are they important to the organization?

  - What requirements or boundaries must the team work within?

  - Do we have the expertise, competencies, and resources necessary to accomplish our goals?

  - What does each team member bring to the team?

- What is the reporting relationship to the sponsor?

- What authority to act or decision-making power does the team carry?

- On what issues is the team expected to consult or inform the chartering agent?

- What deliverables are expected?

- How will the team be measured?

DIRECTION EXERCISE NO. 1
Project or Task Team
New Team Charter

Workout Plan

A Midwest manufacturing manager reported only one glitch in his carefully planned team chartering meeting. He assumed that because everyone on the new team knew each other, they would know why each person was on the new team.

His advice: When people have worked together and lived in the same community for years, be sure to clearly state what each member brings to the team, why each is important to the team's success. This helps team members let go of old perceptions and create a positive working relationship for the new team.

When to use
At the first meeting of a new special project team

Time
30 to 60 minutes

Materials
Agenda made from chartering topics page, summary worksheet

Purpose/objectives

- Start up the first project team meeting with clear, structured information.

- Make certain that basic team expectations and scope of responsibilities are clear and shared by all team members.

- Proactively answer questions that help create a context for teamwork.

- Provide opportunity for team members to clarify areas of uncertainty.

Grouping
All project team members and sponsor

Warm-up
Welcome all team members. Plan a short activity to help team members get to know one another better.

- If members have not met, have them share information about themselves that others need to know.

- If members know one another, share one thing others would be unlikely to know, such as one memory from before the age of 10 or the like.

- In all instances, have everyone share their ideas on why they were chosen to be on this team.

Aerobics

1. Give general project information if needed.

2. Introduce the sponsor. (This person needs the chartering questions in advance to prepare thoughtful comments.) The main agenda belongs to the sponsor. Move through the agenda in an interactive way.

3. Provide a question/answer time for questions of any kind about the project.

Cooldown

After the sponsor finishes the agenda, he or she is free to leave. The team debriefs by summarizing and agreeing on key points made, and recording them for future use on the chartering summary sheet. The team may wish to move on to other fitness exercises, such as those suggested in Appendix B.

NOTE

The sponsor is the person who puts the team into being, to whom the team is accountable, and who is officially responsible for the team.

DIRECTION INFORMATION SHEET—EXERCISE NO.1

New team chartering meeting

Key topics for agenda

1. Overview of project scope and definition

   • Underlying purpose of the project

   • Scope and expected outcomes

   • Key processes for which the team is responsible

2. Why the project is important to the organization

   Why the project is important to team members (the business case)

   Why each team member was selected for the project

3. Background information/situation explanation

4. Customer information/requirements/needs

5. Team expectations

   • Autonomy/authority
   Who and when to consult/inform

   • Expected deliverables

   • Timeline

   • Resources

   • Boundaries/restraints

   • How the team will be measured

Direction Worksheet—Exercise No. 1
Chartering meeting summary sheet

Team: _____

Date: _____

Sponsor: _____

1. Key processes for which the team is responsible

   • _____

   • _____

   • _____

   • _____

   • _____

2. Expected deliverables or work output

   • _____

   • _____

   • _____

   • _____

   • _____

3. Key measures of team's work

    *   _____

    *   _____

    *   _____

    *   _____

    *   _____

4. Expectations for how to work (such as givens, boundaries, considerations, and the like)

    *   _____

    *   _____

    *   _____

    *   _____

    *   _____

DIRECTION EXERCISE NO. 2
Long-Term or Ongoing Team Chartering Meeting

Workout Plan

When to use
At any time an existing team needs to clarify its charter or boundaries. Organizations change and emphasis changes. Sometimes it is useful to revisit the team's original purpose to determine if its scope and boundaries have changed as well.

Time
60 to 90 minutes

Materials
Chartering questions worksheet, one overhead transparency of the exercise worksheet

Purpose/objectives

- Anticipate and answer questions that help create a critical context for teamwork.

- Provide opportunity for team members to clarify areas of uncertainty.

- Make certain that basics of team expectations are clear and shared by all members of the team.

Grouping
All team members and sponsor

Warm-up
Clarify for team members how the charter fits into developing clear direction for the team and the importance of clear boundaries to individuals as they go about the work of the team.

Aerobics

1. Hand out the chartering questions worksheet.

2. Each team member independently reads the chartering questions and marks an X by the *two* questions they would like to have clarified.

3. Record on the transparency each member's marks and discover where there is the most interest. Questions with the most marks become the agenda for the meeting. Do as many as there are marks for, or as many as you have time for, but proceed in sequence starting with the ones that got the most marks.

4. The heart of the meeting is working through the questions about which members are most unclear, and holding an interactive discussion with the sponsor to gain clarity and understanding.

Cooldown

After the sponsor finishes the agenda, he or she is free to leave. The team debriefs by summarizing and agreeing on key points made, and recording them for future use. This is a good time to discuss the positioning of the team, its goals, and objectives.

Where are we on-track? What changes must be made in our work? In our thinking?

Chartering Questions Worksheet—Exercise No. 2

Mark with an X the two questions *you* would most like answered.

- What processes is this team responsible for and why are they important to the organization?
  _____
  _____

- What requirements or boundaries must the team work within?
  _____
  _____

- Do we have the expertise, competencies, and resources necessary to accomplish our goals?
  _____
  _____

- What does each team member bring to the team?
  _____
  _____

- What is the reporting relationship to the sponsor?
  _____
  _____

- What authority to act or decision-making power does the team carry?
  _____
  _____

- On what issues is the team expected to consult or inform the chartering agent?
  _____
  _____

- What deliverables are expected?
  _____
  _____

- How will the team be measured?
  _____
  _____

DIRECTION FACTOR NO. 2
Vision

Definition: Vision is the mental image of your team's ideal. It is the process of looking to the future and creating the most desirable scenario for your team.

About visioning

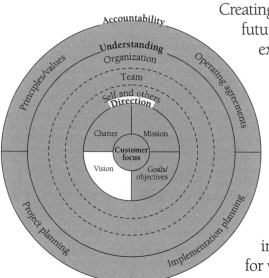

Creating a vision is the process of building a desired scenario for the future. It requires getting outside the day-to-day perspective, examining your organization from an external perspective, and deciding what your team could look like, how it would operate, and what it would be doing at its optimum. Creating your vision is, at its best, a shared process and one that can generate enthusiasm and commitment for you and your team members.

The team vision tells or shows what the team would ultimately like to become. The purpose of the vision is to free up and liberate team members from the routine and imperfection of present operations, and to create an inspiration for what to make come true.

If you want commitment to your team's vision, it must be shared with as many people as possible. The more stake your team members have in the formulation of the vision, the more committed they will be to the accomplishment of it, and the more they will be able to take the necessary risks.

Visioning actions

Visioning actions usually are creative activities using words, pictures, or metaphors to illustrate members' aspirations for the team. Working from each member's individual vision, the team collectively builds a shared vision that incorporates aspects from all members.

Visioning questions

- How might we be working five years from now?

- If our customers were wildly happy with our work, what would they be saying about us?

- What would it be like if we were working to our optimum as a team?

- What would we create or contribute to our organization and our customers?

Our dream.

DIRECTION EXERCISE NO. 3
A One-Day Visioning Meeting

Workout Plan

When to use
With a team that wants to look ahead and create a consensus-based desired future. To provide an end-state to which to aspire.

Time
1 day (8 hours)

Materials
Flip chart, colored markers

Purpose/objectives

What would our best look like?

- To use the collective memory and perceptions of team members to build one shared vision

- To allow all team members to take an active part in writing the vision.

- To honor and validate successes from the past and to pull them with us into the future

Grouping
Small to large group—up to 30 or so

Warm-up
Introduction: Answer these questions.

Why visioning? How does it fit for us now?

Visioning—What is it about? How does it work? How will it benefit us?

To warm up, start with a short influences activity: Each individual draws symbols or pictures of things, events, trends that have influenced them in the last five years or so. Draw in three parts: individually—at the workplace—in the world.

Drawings are hung all around the room and people have time to quietly walk around and look at several drawings or to engage others in telling about their drawings. This is time to synthesize and draw from other people's thinking and experiences.

Aerobics

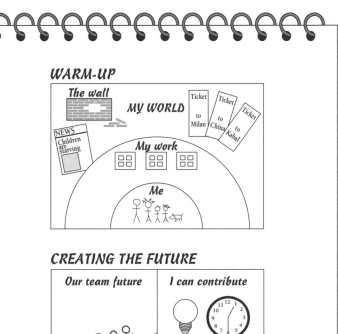

1. Creating the future
   Each person receives a new sheet of flip chart paper. Fold it in half or draw a line down the middle. Draw or symbolize the preferred future for the organization on one half of the paper, and on the other half symbolize something each personally can contribute to help make that vision become reality.

   In groups of five or six, each person takes four to five minutes to explain his/her drawings.

2. Meaning making
   Each participant summarizes the previous experience in writing.

   a. Build. Some things I feel are the heart of the vision—priorities to continue or on which to build

   b. Minimize. Some things I would like to minimize or let go of as we move into the future

3. Determining themes and shared ideas
   Original groups meet to briefly share and to develop a list of themes or areas of shared ideas they find in their Build and Minimize lists. Each group then writes a Common Themes list for both Build and Minimize—a list to which they all agree.

Build lists are posted in one area and Minimize lists are posted in a second area.

Groups look at all lists to identify themes and shared ideas from group to group—particularly in the Build lists. Clarify that a group vision contains some compromise and melding of other people's thinking, so it will be different from our own individual vision.

4. Building a vision statement
Form new groups of five or six at this point and use the same steps identified for building a mission statement (worksheet for Exercise No. 6 in this section) to make one vision statement from each group. Then collectively make it into one statement from the entire group.

(Depending on group size and time constraints, this may be too cumbersome for all to participate. In that case, appoint a spokesperson from each group to build the vision based on the input received. This statement can be finalized later and agreed upon by all team members.)

Cooldown
Write the final or draft statement on a flip chart. Team members may wish to sign it when it is completed. Decide what the team wants to do with its new vision. Who should be told? Where should it be displayed? How will it be used to drive decision making?

DIRECTION EXERCISE NO. 4
Warm-Up Vision

Workout Plan

When to use
To prepare for writing a mission statement or conducting a goal setting session. To get people started thinking about the team's vision and/or mission.

Time
1 hour

Materials
Flip chart paper, markers, masking tape

Purpose/objectives

- Warm up team members and get the creative process started.

- Move past the daily reality to look at the team's work in a little more lofty or higher purpose perspective.

- Provide a point of reference that the team is working toward.

- Guide the development of the team's mission or goals with its longer term purpose for being.

Grouping
Entire team

How we made it happen.

Warm-up
Have team members close their eyes and imagine that today is _____, 19___ (three or four years from now). On this day, "60 Minutes" TV program is filming to profile our team as an example of excellence in our field. Take a few minutes to imagine what is going on as the day, the interviews, and filming begin.

Example: Repro department—what our direct customers would say

*"*I don't know how they do it! I've been over there three times in the last week with a rush, not easy jobs either, and each time they called me to come pick it up early. Once when they couldn't make it on time they called me, very apologetically to ask for an extra 10 minutes to finish. WOW! That's attention to detail! And when the job's done, it's right—not crooked on the page, or half printed. Besides, every time Diana, the order clerk, sees me coming her face lights up like I was her best friend, not her next rush job. I've been coming here for repro help for two years now and it's always like that. They must be on some great stress management program or something!"

Aerobics

1. Divide the team into small groups. Assign each group an identity.

   Group 1—our direct customers

   Group 2—our sponsor/chartering agent

   Group 3—our team members

   Group 4—a key stakeholder group

   Group 5—the end users of our product or services
   (Use as many groups as make sense for your team size and purpose.)

2. Assign the groups the following task.
   Pretend you are this group and you are being interviewed about the success of our team and what we did that made it all happen.

   Give specific quotes. What were the ingredients? What behaviors? What heroic acts? How did we overcome obstacles? What made us stand out in your minds?

   What is it we would like to hear these groups (and ourselves) say about us?

Cooldown

1. At the end of the 30-minute time, each group reports their quotes to the larger team. After the reports, give team members a chance to respond to the feeling the reports created. Is energy up? What energized you? Which part struck a chord for you personally?

2. Make the tie to the next step—developing the mission statement or goals. Visioning gets us energized and looking to the future creatively and toward how we would like to be seen. The mission statement will focus us and make sure all our actions are taking us toward that vision. Goal setting will focus our daily actions on results.

DIRECTION EXERCISE NO. 5
Creating a Team Vision—with Pictures

Workout Plan

When to use
You want to create a vision for your organization. You want to lift your sights from the everyday and explore what you could build in the future. Using pictures may be more adventuresome than using words. We find that it unleashes the creative spirit and provides a lot more fun to the process. Some people will be timid. Assure them you are not looking for art, but ideas.

Time
4 hours

Materials
Flip chart paper and markers for each person

Purpose/objectives

- To create a vision for the team that builds commitment

- To tap the creative expertise of all team members

Grouping
Every member of the team

Warm-up
Describe the need for a vision as a guide to daily decisions and as encouragement for risk taking. Suggest that people close their eyes and listen quietly to the questions that follow. Read the questions to stimulate their thinking. Ask them to jot down notes to themselves on what the team might look like if it were performing ideally.

Aerobics

1. Give each person flip chart paper and colored markers to draw a picture of their vision for the team or organization. The only rules are,

> **A** new CEO attended the Executive Development Institute in 1986. At that time he was challenged to create a vision for his statewide division. He pretended to write the cover story for *Fortune* magazine. Six years later, he reported that everything he wrote was now true and even more profitable than he had imagined. Only one thing from his cover story had yet to be achieved—his description of himself, writing away, aboard his yacht in the Caribbean!

"Few if any words, and no organization charts." Give them 20 minutes. Most people will have to think about what they want to draw. Don't be worried if people don't start drawing right away. They are thinking. Suddenly, they will get their idea and start drawing in a spurt.

2. Post these on the wall. Let everyone walk around and look at each other's vision.

3. Let each member come forward and explain his or her drawing.

4. Ask, "What did you like about _____'s ideas?" "What is a new idea that we want to keep?" Move through each vision drawing.

5. Ask each person to write a short statement of the vision. (An alternative method is to cut the pictures and combine them with transparent tape, making sure that a portion of each person's drawing is in the composite. Then ask them to write down what the composite means.)

6. Our task now is to create a combined vision which represents the best thoughts of each of us. If the group is small (less than six people), do this in one group. If it is larger, divide into smaller groups and ask each to write a vision statement that incorporates the best thinking of all the team members.

7. Post on the wall. Ask, "Is this us? Is this what we want to become?" When you have reached agreement on the vision statement, ask each person to come forward and sign his or her name as a symbol of their commitment to the vision.

Cooldown
Decide what you want to do with the new vision. How will you keep it before you in your daily work? (Some groups make a poster, laminated wallet cards, or desk tents, or put their vision picture in the common room.)

DIRECTION INFORMATION SHEET—EXERCISE NO. 5

Vision exercise prework

Vision think questions

Please spend some time individually thinking through these questions in preparation for our session to build a shared vision.

Focus on the customer

  1. Who is our customer, the receiver of our work?

  2. How will they be doing business in the future?

  3. How can we contribute to their business' success?

Focus on our team or organization

  4. How should we be doing business?

  5. What kinds of products and services should we provide?

  6. How do we want the organization and/or community to see us?

  7. Where do we provide expertise that others don't have?

Focus on the stakeholders (anyone who has an interest in the output of this team)

  8. What do they get from their investment in our team?

  9. What makes them proud to be a stakeholder with us?

Focus on the systems we need to have in place

  10. What technology and technical expertise do we need?

  11. What kind of partnering or supplier relationships do we want to create?

DIRECTION FACTOR NO. 3
Mission

Definition: A mission statement is a brief, concise statement which defines the business you are in, for whom, and why. It is your purpose and reason for existence and it defines your unique contribution.

About mission statements

The mission statement clarifies from each member's point of view the focus and direction of the team. Accomplishing the mission of the team should take the team toward its vision. The mission statement should be somewhat uplifting but more practical and here and now than the vision, and should be no more than a paragraph in length. Only team members should be involved in its development. The purpose of the mission statement is for each member to be very clear on what the team is about. Each member can then make independent decisions when necessary, knowing that each person's decisions will help the team move in the right direction. Therefore, a clear consensus process and opportunity for discussion are essential to writing a useful mission statement.

Mission actions

The mission statement process generally is a structured, step-by-step process of brainstorming key words and phrases; collecting them via round robin from team members; discussing and clarifying ideas and concepts; then drafting statements until one is agreed upon by the entire team.

Mission statement questions

- What is our unique contribution to the organization, that would not be happening if we did not exist?

- Who is our customer—to whom do we deliver our outputs?

- What are the interests/priorities of our customer?

- What are the boundaries (organizational or geographic) within which we operate?

- How would we like to be seen by our customers—or to be known within the organization?

DIRECTION EXERCISE NO. 6
Mission Statement

Workout Plan

When to use
With new or existing long-term teams or project teams to target individual actions toward the common goal. To help teams get to the root cause of their reason for being.

Time
2 to 4 hours

Materials
Be sure to give out prework questions in advance. Flip charts (2) and markers, mission exercise worksheets

Purpose/objectives

- Create a mission statement, approximately a paragraph long.

- Generate input from all team members in building the mission statement so there is buy-in for the completed statement.

Grouping
Entire team (If you have more than 10 or 12 people, this process will be much more complicated and will take longer.)

Warm-up
It may be helpful to do the short visioning exercise as a warm-up to get ready for this activity and to set the context of what we'd like to become as we move forward (see Direction Exercise No. 4).

Aerobics
Follow steps on mission exercise worksheet.

   For larger groups, combine into pairs or groups of three for the earlier steps in order to manage the structure and give everyone input.

Cooldown

When your statement is complete, celebrate! This is a critical step in getting shared understanding that helps individual members work independently while still going straight toward the target your team has set.

NOTE

You may need to stop when you have several drafts. You can appoint a small group to take the drafts and propose back to the team one version that is a combination of the drafts. This is especially helpful for larger teams.

Mission Statement

To foster an environment which promotes teamwork as the funda-mental means by which each employee and *pursue* excellence through quality.

Sample mission statement.

Direction Worksheet—Exercise No. 6

Mission exercise prework

Mission think questions
Please spend some time individually thinking through these questions in preparation for our session to build a shared mission statement.

1. What business is the total organization in? Why does it exist?

   _____

   _____

   _____

2. What business is our division/department in? Why do we exist?

   _____

   _____

   _____

3. What are our principal products/services/functions?

   _____

   _____

   _____

4. How do these products/services/functions contribute to the total organization's roles and missions?

   _____

   _____

   _____

5. What is unique or distinctive about our division's work as compared to other units in the organization?

   _____

   _____

   _____

6. What issues are important and unique about our area (image, leadership, environment, operational strategies, innovations, quality, practices, and so forth)?

   _____

   _____

   _____

Direction Worksheet—Exercise No. 6

Steps to developing a mission statement

Step 1. Individuals think about and write answers to questions 1–4 on their own.

1. What is the unique contribution of this team?

   _____

   _____

2. Who are our key customers (internal and external)?

   _____

   _____

3. What are some values and beliefs that guide our work
   (the kind of team you would like to be known as)?

   _____

   _____

4. Key words: Looking back at questions 1–3, what are some single words that you believe should
   be contained in your team's mission?

   - _____   - _____

   - _____   - _____

   - _____   - _____

   - _____   - _____

Step 2. Key words from each team member are collected round robin (each gives one word in rotation until all words are listed). Words are recorded on flip chart paper and posted for everyone to see.

Step 3. Phrases: Combining some of your words and your team members' words, work in pairs or threesomes to develop three or four short phrases you would propose be included in your team's mission statement.

- _____

- _____

- _____

- _____

Step 4. Key phrases from each pair or threesome are collected round robin (each gives one idea in rotation until all phrases are listed). Phrases are recorded on flip chart paper and posted for everyone to see.

Step 5. Draft statement: Based on discussions with your team members, work in small groups (again, two or three) to draft a two- to three-sentence paragraph that you believe describes the mission of your team. Use all the posted words and phrases to stimulate your thinking, but don't be restricted by them or limited just to using them—new thoughts and phrases are appropriate, too.

_____

_____

_____

Step 6. Tape all drafts to the wall and have each read aloud by someone who did not write that particular draft. Allow each person to then mark two or three things on other people's drafts that they particularly like.

Step 7. Combine parts of drafts or create a new draft with elements of the earlier drafts that all members can buy into. You may need to write and then consider it a few days before finalizing.

DIRECTION EXERCISE NO. 7
Short Mission Statement

Workout Plan

When to use
With a new or existing short-term team to target individual actions toward the common goal. To provide guidance to help team members define the scope of their work.

Time
1 to 2 hours

Materials
Mission statement agenda, mission statement worksheet for each member, flip chart paper and markers, masking tape

Purpose/objectives

- Create a mission statement, one to two sentences long.

- Generate input from all team members in building the mission statement so there is buy-in for the completed statement.

Grouping
All members of the team if the team is small. If larger, divide into groups of four or five each.

Warm-up
Introduce the topic. Ask why team members think a mission statement is important. Tell why the mission statement is important to you.

Aerobics

1. Using the mission statement worksheet, each member writes his or her own mission statement.

2. Each group or person writes their mission statement on flip chart paper and posts it on the wall.

3. Everyone walks around and reads the statements on the wall.

4. Read each person's mission statement aloud, one at a time.

5. Ask, "What special words or ideas do you like in this statement?"
    Underline those words in a different color and move on to the next
    until all are completed.

6. Ask, "How can we merge these into one statement that we can all
    agree upon?"

7. "Is there one that you like especially well?" Choose one that needs
    the least work.

8. "Now, let's add some words and ideas from the other statements that
    can make this one represent all our thinking."

9. After edits, rewrite a clean draft on a new page.

10. Check agreement, "Can we all agree to this mission statement?" If
    yes, let everyone have the opportunity to sign or initial their agree-
    ment. If no, continue to work on the wording until you do get
    agreement.

Cooldown

After developing the mission statement, plan how you will use it. How can
you keep it before you in your daily tasks? How will you share it with others
who may be interested? If the mission statement has been given to a
subgroup for wordsmithing, how will you get together to agree on the final
product?

DIRECTION INFORMATION SHEET—EXERCISE NO. 7

Mission statement—key considerations

A mission statement tells the you and others what business you are in, for whom, and why. It is your purpose, your reason for existence. Hopefully, it distinguishes you from your competition.

The mission statement can be published on your brochures, perhaps your letterhead and cards, and also made clearly visible to all who enter your building. Every team member has responsibility for the accomplishment of the mission.

We may put some things in a mission statement that are not completely accurate at this time, but they are qualities for which we are striving.

It is good for a mission statement to be succinct so that everyone can remember it, usually one or two sentences or a short paragraph. Often it includes the customer and how we can help the customer.

The task for the team is to complete a statement that tells why they exist, what they are to do, and who they serve and for what purpose.

The mission statement answers the questions, "What business are we in? Why do we exist?"

Direction Worksheet—Exercise No. 7

Mission statement

In order to create the mission statement, consider the following:

- Who is our customer?

- What products and services do we provide?

- What do we do for the customer that is unique?

- Why does the customer need us?

At the end of this exercise we should have developed one statement that expresses the collective thoughts of the group.

_____ exists
                                    (organization)

to do what? _____

for whom? _____

why? _____

DIRECTION FACTOR NO. 4
Goals and Objectives

Definitions: Goals are broad strategic statements of what we want to accomplish. Given the mission and vision of the organization, we have to define what the major goals are that will take us toward our vision and help accomplish our mission.

Objectives are tactical. They spell out the specific activities and timeline for what must be undertaken and met in order to accomplish the goals (the what, when, and who).

About goals and objectives

Caution: One of the chief reasons that teams fail is that they frequently begin with goals and objectives without a clear mission and charter. Getting all team members clear on charter, vision, and mission makes the setting of goals and objectives a much more interactive, easy, and effective process.

Goals and objectives actions

Goal-setting activities are meant to tie down what will be accomplished by whom in a certain period of time. With a clear vision and mission the goal-setting activity becomes apparent, and the process flows easily.

Are we aligned?

Goals and objectives questions

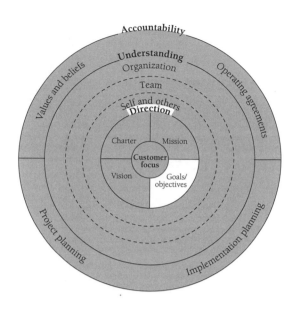

- What are the major things we are to accomplish during this period of time?

- What are the necessary interim steps, the specific objectives that will allow us to accomplish our goals?

- What timelines will we need to assure our goals are accomplished?

- For what will we be held accountable on the next review?

- What is my personal responsibility?

Goal
Develop methods to identify, understand and measure (internal and external) customer needs and expectations.

Objectives
1. Perform a study of methods being used to gather customer information for 20 percent of our identified customer base by end of second quarter.
2. Establish system to record and disseminate customer information from all customer complaint calls and letters, from focus group meetings, and from customer surveys. Pilot in second quarter within West Coast site.
3. Establish five appropriate benchmarks that create a family of measures for each of the top-10 customer requirements by beginning of third quarter.

DIRECTION EXERCISE NO. 8
Goals and Objectives
Top-Down

Workout Plan

When to use
At the appropriate time of the year, usually annually or semiannually with quarterly updates. To allow the team to think through how the work of the team contributes to the overall mission of the enterprise.

Time
1 to 4 hours, depending upon the size of the group

Materials
Copies of corporate strategic plans, corporate and group mission and vision statements, last year's goals and objectives, flip chart paper, marking pens, masking tape, and action plan worksheets

Purpose/objectives

- To develop specific measurable goals and objectives that further the mission and vision for the team and each individual, where applicable

- To develop specific measurable goals and objectives that further the corporate strategic plan

- To deliberate upon strategy for achieving the goals

- To develop specific action plans and strategies for individuals and the team

Grouping
All team members

Warm-up

1. Begin with discussion of the corporate strategy and goals.

2. Discuss the team goals from the previous year.
   What has changed?

Which goals are still relevant?

Which goals need to be updated?

What should new goals look like?

Aerobics

1. Ask each team member to draft three or four goals they feel are the areas the team should focus on for the next period of time. Post these on flip chart paper.

2. Ask, "What are the major themes of these goals? Where do we all agree? If we could choose one special goal for this team, what would it be?"

   Decide on four to five goals for the team.

3. Brainstorm various strategies for achieving these goals.
   Decide on the strategies.

4. List each major goal. Under the goals, list the enabling objectives necessary to accomplish the goals. Use the objective setting worksheet for this. Include the objective, who is responsible, and the date for accomplishment.

Cooldown

Who will be responsible for providing everyone with copies of the team goals? Who needs to communicate the results of today's meeting to other interested parties? Are we satisfied that our goals are important and attainable?

Direction Worksheet—Exercise No. 8
Objective Setting

Major goal:

_____

_____

_____

_____

_____

_____

Objectives	Who	When	How measured
1. _____	_____	_____	_____
_____	_____	_____	_____
_____	_____	_____	_____
2. _____	_____	_____	_____
_____	_____	_____	_____
_____	_____	_____	_____
3. _____	_____	_____	_____
_____	_____	_____	_____
_____	_____	_____	_____
4. _____	_____	_____	_____
_____	_____	_____	_____
_____	_____	_____	_____
5. _____	_____	_____	_____
_____	_____	_____	_____
_____	_____	_____	_____

Major goal:

_____

_____

_____

_____

_____

_____

Objectives	Who	When	How measured
1. _____	_____	_____	_____
_____	_____	_____	_____
_____	_____	_____	_____
2. _____	_____	_____	_____
_____	_____	_____	_____
_____	_____	_____	_____
3. _____	_____	_____	_____
_____	_____	_____	_____
_____	_____	_____	_____
4. _____	_____	_____	_____
_____	_____	_____	_____
_____	_____	_____	_____
5. _____	_____	_____	_____
_____	_____	_____	_____
_____	_____	_____	_____

DIRECTION EXERCISE NO. 9
Bottom-Up Goal Setting

Workout Plan

When to use
This is a proactive goal-setting process that is useful when there is no top-down strategic direction offered, or in areas where there is a strong desire for team autonomy and empowerment, an environment of self-direction. This also works in a strongly customer–supplier oriented enterprise, or when you are the top management team.

Time
2 to 4 hours, depending on size of group

Materials
Goals and objectives from the previous time period (last quarter, last six months, and so forth), bigger picture organizational goals, objectives, strategies, visions for the future

Purpose/objectives

- Provide guidance for daily actions for each team member.

- Ensure that actions and activities of team members are contributing to achieving the desired direction of the team.

- Clarify responsibilities between team members while creating synergy and support for common causes.

Grouping
Entire team

Warm-up
Do a one-hour visioning warm-up (Direction Exercise No. 4) to set a vision for the next year, or review a previously set vision for the team.

Aerobics

1. Each team member focuses on his or her own responsibilities, goals, and objectives for the period just past. Using that understanding of past activities that support the team, and the vision for the team's preferred future, each member writes suggested goals and objectives for themselves for the coming period.

2. Team members pair up and coach each other, listening and offering suggestions to strengthen and fine tune the goals and objectives originally written by each.

3. Each member presents suggested goals and objectives to the team for further input.

4. After individual goals and objectives are finalized, the team writes collective goals and objectives that represent the overall work of the team.

Cooldown

If you are the top management team, plan how you will communicate these goals to others in your enterprise. Plan how you can gain buy-in from others. If you are one team in a larger company, the team leader or manager presents team goals to the sponsor for validation or redirection, and to be incorporated into the goal setting for the larger organization.

Direction Worksheet—Exercise No. 9

Action planning worksheet

	What?	Who?	When?	How measured?
1.				
2.				
3.				
4.				
5.				
6.				
7.				
8.				
9.				
10.				

DIRECTION EXERCISE NO. 10
Which Goals Have Priority?

Workout Plan

When to use
During the goal-setting process. This may come at the conclusion of building your vision, at the beginning of your new planning process, or when there is confusion about team goals. Sometimes goals are accomplished simultaneously; sometimes, the accomplishment of one goal depends on the completion of another one. This process helps the team to sequence goals, allocate resources, and decide which goals can wait, if push comes to shove.

Time
1 hour

Materials
Goal priority worksheets, weighted pairs worksheets, flip charts, marking pens

Purpose/objectives

- To prioritize the team's goals in relation to how well they support the vision or mission

- To prioritize the goals according to their value to the team and the company

Grouping
All team members

Warm-up
Pass out goal priority worksheets and weighted pairs worksheets.

Which goals have priority?

Aerobics

1. Team members compare goals by asking the question, "If I have to make a choice in terms of 'most important' to the team achieving success, my choice is (one of the two)." You will be comparing all goals to each other, two at a time.

2. After all goals are compared with each other, find the total times each goal is circled and record at the bottom of the page.

    This part of the exercise may be done all together as a group or individually, with the totals placed on a flip chart made to look like the weighted pairs worksheet.

3. Reorder or sequence the goals according to the results.

Cooldown
Allow time for everyone to study the results.

- Where is there agreement?

- Where is there divergence? On the goals where there is strong disagreement, ask for discussion.

Come to consensus on the priority of the various goals to the team.

Goal Priority Worksheet—Exercise No. 10

List the goals for this team.

1. _____
   _____
   _____

2. _____
   _____
   _____

3. _____
   _____
   _____

4. _____
   _____
   _____

5. _____
   _____
   _____

6. _____
   _____
   _____

7. _____
   _____
   _____

8. _____
   _____
   _____

9. _____
   _____
   _____

Direction Worksheet—Exercise No. 10
Weighted pairs

Instructions: Compare each goal to every other goal. Which of each of these two goals is more important to team success?

Number of times each goal is circled:

1 2	1 3	1 4	1 5	1 6	1 7	1 8	1 9
	2 3	2 4	2 5	2 6	2 7	2 8	2 9
		3 4	3 5	3 6	3 7	3 8	3 9
			4 5	4 6	4 7	4 8	4 9
				5 6	5 7	5 8	5 9
					6 7	6 8	6 9
						7 8	7 9
							8 9

Goal 1 _____

Goal 2 _____

Goal 3 _____

Goal 4 _____

Goal 5 _____

Goal 6 _____

Goal 7 _____

Goal 8 _____

Goal 9 _____

List new priority for goals.

1. _____   6. _____

2. _____   7. _____

3. _____   8. _____

4. _____   9. _____

5. _____

Goal Priority Worksheet—Exercise No. 10

Team: *Total quality supplier relationship project team*

List the goals for this team.

1. *Establish a set of key suppliers with whom TQM concepts will be implemented.*

2. *Investigate the feasibility of a partnership arrangement with suppliers.*

3. *Establish and implement a system for providing feedback on performance to suppliers.*

4. *Establish and implement a system for measuring supplier performance.*

5. *Define an approach for achieving an appropriate level of risk-sharing by our suppliers.*

6. *Develop and issue a standard specification which establishes our TQM concepts and our expectations of suppliers.*

Example of team goals to prioritize.

Direction Worksheet—Exercise No. 10
Weighted pairs

Instructions: Compare each goal to every other goal. Which of each of these two goals is more important to team success?

each goal is circled:

Number of times

```
①  ①  ①  ①  ①  1  1  1      Goal 1 __5__
2   3   4   5   6   7  8  9

    2   2   ②  2   2  2  2    Goal 2 __1__
    ③  ④  5   ⑥  7  8  9

        3   ③  3   3  3  3    Goal 3 __2__
        ④  5   ⑥  7  8  9

            ④  4   4  4  4    Goal 4 __3__
            5   ⑥  7  8  9

                5   5  5  5    Goal 5 __0__
                ⑥  7  8  9

                    6  6  6    Goal 6 __4__
                    7  8  9

                       7  7    Goal 7 _____
                       8  9

                          8    Goal 8 _____

                          9    Goal 9 _____
```

List new priority for goals.

1. **Key suppliers**   6. **Risk-taking**

2. **Standard specs**   7.

3. **Measuring system**   8.

4. **Feedback system**   9.

5. **Partnership**

Example of reprioritized goals.

Fitness Area III:
Understanding Exercises

Definition: To be able to see, understand, and interpret the inherent nature of ourselves, our team members, our organization.

About understanding

When the team is clear about its direction, much productivity and commitment can be gained by working together to gain increased understanding. Team members see each other as unique individuals and see the strength that comes from the diversity of team members. They understand the power and synergy of a team that has balance in viewpoints and can see a situation, opportunity, or problem from many different sides. They coach and help each team member to be their most successful. They can effectively use the organizational systems and informal political network within their company to help achieve team goals.

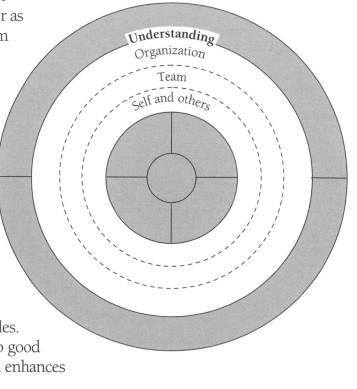

Understanding actions

Activities that increase team member understanding can be diverse. Self studies can help members become more conscious of their own work preferences and styles. Learning about group process builds skills necessary to good group working habits. Understanding the organization enhances the implementation and acceptance of the team's work.

Understanding questions

- Do I know myself and my teammates in a way that lets us tap into our different styles and unique talents?

- How does this team need to be like and different from other teams in order to be most effective?

- Do we use the most effective and efficient ways for teams to operate in the system and culture of our overall organization?

Exercises in this section

- Understanding Factor No. 1: Self and Others

    1. In-Depth Intros

    2. What Makes Us Tick?

    3. How Do I Use My Time?

- Understanding Factor No. 2: Team

    4. Are We a Team or Workgroup?

    5. Observing Individual Behaviors in Teamwork

    6. Consensus Decision Making

    7. What Sport?

    8. Ten-Minute Team Process

    9. Process Check

    10. Box and Bubble

    11. Leadership Transition Meeting

    12. Best Boss

- Understanding Factor No. 3: Organization

    13. Culture Audit

    14. Culture Observation

UNDERSTANDING FACTOR NO. 1
Self and Others

Definition: Understanding of self and others and how individual differences and behaviors either support or take away from team effectiveness.

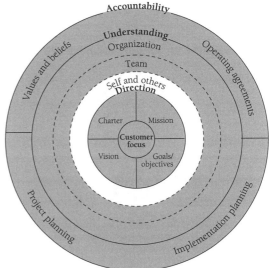

About understanding self and others

Understanding yourself is the first step in understanding and valuing others who are different from you. In this section we examine how we prefer to work, and how certain behaviors can help move the team effectiveness beyond individualistic behaviors.

Understanding self and others actions

The team can explore each member's background of experience and share information on priorities, talents, and preferences to develop an understanding of how to work with each other. Over a period of time, the team can use this understanding of each individual to help increase everyone's ability to work as a team.

Understanding self and others questions

- What strengths and preferences do I bring to the team? What are my rough edges and development needs?

- What resources can I offer other team members or tap into from other team members?

Understanding yourself is the first step to understanding others.

UNDERSTANDING EXERCISE NO. 1
In-Depth Intros

Workout Plan

When to use
At the beginning of any new grouping (in other words, a new team, or a new committee).

Strength comes from diverse ideas, competencies, backgrounds, and styles.

Time
30 to 60 minutes

Materials
Flip chart paper, worksheet

Purpose/objectives

- To get to know each other in-depth and quickly

- To begin to build a common language and camaraderie

- To discover the expertise of team members

Grouping
Entire team

Warm-up
Ask team members to pair up and talk through the topics on the topics list. Give them five minutes each.

Aerobics

1. Each person introduces his or her partner to the rest of the group. Set a time limit based on the number of people in the group. (This exercise can take up to 30 minutes, but will save hours in the long run because you will get everyone's background out in front of the group all at one time.)

2. Ask someone to be the timekeeper and to blow the whistle, tap the glass, and so forth, when the time is up for each introduction.

3. Members make notes about each team member on the In-Depth Intros summary worksheet.

Cooldown

Debrief: Ask questions that include each member who was introduced. "This is a quiz. Who likes to ride a bicycle on cross-country trips? Who is going back to school in the next year?" Or request comments from the group. What surprised you? What pleased you? Did you notice any common themes?

UNDERSTANDING INFORMATION SHEET— EXERCISE NO. 1

Team introduction topics

- What is the name you prefer to be called? (Some people are called by names they prefer not to be called, or will have stories about names they're called by friends and family.)

- What do you get paid to do? (This is not a job description. It could be something like, "go to meetings so you can work in peace," or "to think and be creative," or "protect the boss from intruders.")

- What are your positive hot buttons? (Something you would like to talk about if we ran into each other informally, such as a sport you like, travel, or kids.)

- What are your negative hot buttons? (Something that makes you angry, irritated, makes you see red, such as sexist jokes, or people who say, "I can't.")

- What specific expertise do you think you bring to this team?

- What is one personal accomplishment you are pleased with in the past year?

- What is one recent professional accomplishment?

- Please share one or some of your objectives for the next year.

If you want to get more personal or have plenty of time, you can add the following topics:

- The best year of my life

- The worst year of my life

- Why I think I was chosen for this team (new member)

- Something no one in this room would know about me

- A turning point in my life

Understanding Worksheet—Exercise No. 1
In-depth intro summary sheet

Preferred name	Paid to do	Hot button +	Hot button -	Expertise

Understanding Worksheet—Exercise No. 1
In-depth intro summary sheet

Personal accomplish-ments	Professional accomplish-ments	Objective	Objective	Other

UNDERSTANDING EXERCISE NO. 2
What Makes Us Tick?

Workout Plan

When to use
You want to learn more about yourself and your fellow teammates.

Time
1 to 2 hours (depending on the size of your team)

Materials
What Makes Us Tick? worksheet

Purpose/objectives

- To provide a way for team members to share things about themselves that are not observable and that have an impact on how members react to each others' actions

- To allow team members to discuss their own characteristics and look for ways to support each other

Grouping
Entire team, but no more than eight or 10. If the team is larger, are there subgroupings that would be workable?

Warm-up
Explain the purpose of the exercise. This is also a good place to include a couple of cartoons that gently remind us of our humanness. The benefit from this session is the candor of team member descriptions. Therefore, it is important to set the scene in a way that can best happen. Should this be held off-site? In a relaxed atmosphere with couches and soft chairs? What timing is best? Allow time for members to think about and fill out the worksheet (or give it as prework before the meeting, but just as an option).

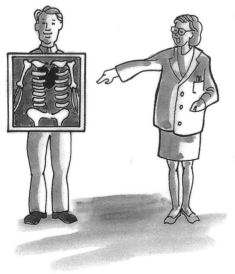

What makes us tick?

Aerobics

1. Go around the group one question at a time (round robin) allowing each person to share her or his responses to the questions. Allow time for clarification and some reaction/discussion as each person shares so that this is interactive and animated, not teachy.

2. After all have responded to a question, ask the group to discuss

   - What did you hear in common with particular team members?

   - Were there areas where what one team member would value, another would not?

   - What suggestions would you have for ways to honor each member's needs and desires?

Cooldown

Ask the team to synthesize by reflecting on the many differences expressed in the session. How can these different ways to see the world be used as an asset for the team? How can they become strengths that differentiate this team from others?

Understanding Worksheet—Exercise No. 2
What makes us tick?

Team members finish the following sentence starters going around the group for each question (round robin).

1. What is important to me in the next 6 months is . . . .

    _____

2. I feel very confident that . . . .

    _____

    I'm not as confident that . . . .

    _____

3. The team can help me by . . . .

    _____

4. I am very open to . . . .

    _____

    I am not so open to . . . .

    _____

5. I want to take some risks on . . . .

    _____

6. If you see me doing something you think is a mistake, please . . . .

    _____

7. If we have conflict, a good way to handle it with me is to . . . .

    _____

    because . . . .

    _____

8. I would appreciate . . . .

    _____

UNDERSTANDING EXERCISE NO. 3
How Do I Use My Time?

Workout Plan

When to use
After a team project has been underway for a short time, or after the first part of a new cycle for setting and completing goals.

Time
2 hours

Materials
How Do I Use My Time? worksheet

Purpose/objectives

How do I use my time?

- To reconcile time spent in various activities not just with activities and time, but also with the team's mission and values

- Balancing various roles by prioritizing activities according to both the efficiency of activities and the effectiveness of relationships and approaches

- To use desired results and the movement toward a desired end as a means to making appropriate decisions on best uses of time

Grouping
Individual activity with group sharing

Warm-up
Each team member keeps a log of time spent in activities for one week

Aerobics

1. Team members work in pairs for 45 minutes to compare time logs and analyze, using the worksheet. Emphasis is on comparing how time actually is used, compared to priorities or compared to team goals and individual objectives.

2. Each individual sets one or two goals for how to improve their own weekly use of time in a way that takes the team more directly toward their goals, mission, and vision.

3. Each pair agrees on one or two key learnings from the analysis.

Cooldown

Each pair shares their key learnings with the entire team. The team and individuals then set one or two goals for more effective weekly use of team time to achieve the team's goals, mission, and vision.

Understanding Worksheet—Exercise No. 3
How do I use my time?

Instructions: Fill in the log by writing time periods, descriptions of activities, and then the appropriate activity type for each activity. Activity types given here are examples. Make up the categories that would be most useful to your team.

Team: _____

Date: _____

Activity types:

Team goals/objectives	Cultural/marketing networking
My responsibility—priorities	Communication/coordination
Administrative	Planning
Customer contact	Other
Mission–vision–build future	

Time	Activity	Activity type
Examples:		
2 hours	Lead project	Goals/objectives
1 hour	Attend briefing	Planning

UNDERSTANDING FACTOR NO. 2
Team

Definition: Understanding the dynamics that make up the collective identity of the team in order to establish effective ways to work collaboratively.

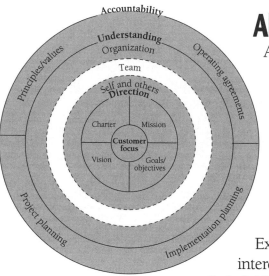

About understanding your team

A team is more than just a collection of individuals. Teams can be very different from one another. The roles that individuals play in groups can have positive or negative influences on teamwork, and can impact overall team results. Understanding the type of teamwork that is most effective for your team for certain situations is critical to effective teamwork

Understanding your team actions

Exercises that help team members explore their relationships and interdependencies and how leadership occurs within the team are helpful for getting a strong understanding of team dynamics.

Understanding your team questions

- What roles do different team members play and how are those roles critical to our success as a team?

- As we work together, what human dynamics allow us to be more successful or less successful as a team?

- What do we need from our leader and how can we influence the leadership of our team?

- How should our team work together in various situations?

UNDERSTANDING EXERCISE NO. 4
Are We a Team or a Work Group?

Workout Plan

When to use
When you want to create awareness of the characteristics of an effective team. You also may be a work group instead of a team, and that may be appropriate for your situation.

Time
30 minutes

Materials
Worksheet, flip chart paper, and marking pens

Purpose/objectives

- To identify whether we are or need to be a team or a work group in order to best meet our goals

- To examine some ways that we might improve our work together

Grouping
Entire team

Warm-up
Discuss the benefits of looking at the team through the eyes of outsiders. Studying how the work flows, how team members work together, and looking at the team's objectives, will help determine if the team is acting as a team (collaborative group, dependent on one another, and working interactively) or work group (loose collection of individuals united on the organization chart). There is nothing wrong with being a work group, if that is the nature of the work flow. It is important for the team to determine the places where a work group is sufficient, and the places where there is a benefit to teaming.

Teams outscore individuals.

Pass out the Team vs. Work Group worksheet.

Aerobics

1. Each person reads a question to him/herself, and answers *team* if the group works as a team, or *work group* if the members work individually.

2. After everyone has read and responded to the worksheet, ask the following with each question.

   a. How many said team or work group?

   b. Give an example of why you answered that way.

   c. Could we and should we become more of a team in this area?

   d. How? For what purpose? How would it be beneficial?

Cooldown

After the discussion is finished, ask if there are any action items the team should take as a result of the discussion. List them and the measures that would indicate performance in that area.

Understanding Worksheet—Exercise No. 4
Team or work group worksheet

Characteristics of effective teams:*

1. Do we have a common goal?

2. Is our goal compelling enough to create a team identity?

3. Is our structure appropriate to our task?

4. Are we capable of collaborating with each other?

5. Do we require coordination to reach our goals?

6. Is the team goal a higher priority than individual goals?

7. Is our personal success achieved through the team's success?

8. Do we have a set of common values?

9. Is the reward system tied to team performance?

10. Do we exert pressure on ourselves to improve the team's performance?

*Adapted from C. Larson and F. LaFasto, *Team Effectiveness.* (Newbury Park, Calif.: Sage Publishing, 1991).

UNDERSTANDING EXERCISE NO. 5
Observing Individual Behaviors in Teamwork

Workout Plan

When to use
To improve the way individuals contribute in meetings

Time
90 minutes

Materials
Worksheets for each team member

Purpose/objectives

- Increase ability to identify and use team process skills that enable team members to participate effectively in group problem solving and decision-making activities

Grouping
Entire team (six to 10 members). If you are doing this with a larger group, subdivide into groups of six to 10 members.

Warm-up
Introduce the concepts of content and process and explain the difference.

Content is what is being worked on.
Process is how that work gets done.

This exercise will focus on the dynamics of how people communicate with each other—that is, how information gets on the table, how people interact with each other, how people are or are not included and how action is taken on information.

Explain that there are three kinds of behaviors that people use as they work on teams.

1. Behaviors that help accomplish the work (*task behaviors*)
      Example: Summarize progress.

2. Behaviors that help maintain the group's cohesiveness (*maintenance behaviors*)
      Example: Ask another's opinion.

3. Behaviors that get in the way (*self behaviors*)
      Example: Belittle another team member's idea.

Explain that the purpose of the activity is to recognize those different behaviors and get an understanding of how individuals on the team work together.

NOTE
You can use any task where the group needs to come to agreement, or accomplish a goal. It should be timed. We frequently use a consensus exercise (see Consensus Decision Making, Understanding Exercise No. 6). You can make up an easy exercise by cutting out some piece of information from a newspaper, such as the one we have included. Team members are to decide their own opinions first and then come to agreement on team answers.

Aerobics

1. Conduct the exercise (See workout plan for Understanding Exercise No. 6).

2. After scoring and debriefing the exercise, turn to the behavior lists. Ask team members to identify specific behaviors and recall specific quotes for each of the kinds of behaviors listed for *task, maintenance,* and *self.* Many team members can give examples of their own behaviors. This is preferred. They also can give examples of teammates' behaviors. You should carefully observe during the exercise and make notes so that you have an example to offer if no one else can think of one for each category.

3. Work through all three sheets in this way, describing the behaviors people recall from the exercise.

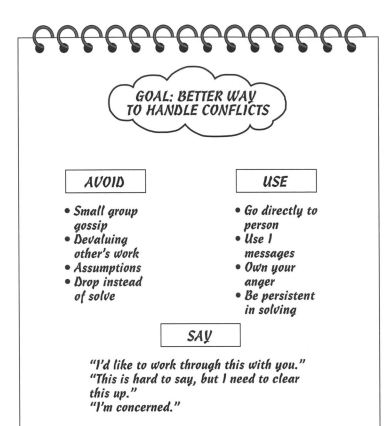

GOAL: BETTER WAY TO HANDLE CONFLICTS

AVOID

- Small group gossip
- Devaluing other's work
- Assumptions
- Drop instead of solve

USE

- Go directly to person
- Use I messages
- Own your anger
- Be persistent in solving

SAY

"I'd like to work through this with you."
"This is hard to say, but I need to clear this up."
"I'm concerned."

Cooldown
Debrief: Think back to all the examples given.

1. What kinds of behaviors were most common?

2. What kinds of behaviors are missing or are used infrequently?

3. If we could set one or two goals for increased effectiveness in behaviors, what would they be?

NOTE

In most teams, task behaviors are most prominent and maintenance behaviors are least prominent. Most teams can identify their self-behaviors easily. This exercise opens a way for those to be talked about in a nonpunitive way and for new agreement or goals to be set to get rid of bad habits that come about naturally to most teams if no attention is paid to this area.

Understanding Worksheet—Exercise No. 5
Understanding behaviors that help accomplish the task

Instructions: Think back to the activity you and your team just completed. Write quotes and specific examples that show how you and your teammates displayed the following kinds of behaviors.

Initiating—proposing; building on another's ideas; suggesting

_____

_____

_____

_____

Seeking information or opinions—requesting facts; asking for suggestions

_____

_____

_____

_____

Giving information or opinions—offering facts or information; stating a belief;

_____

_____

_____

_____

Clarifying and elaborating—clearing up confusion, defining terms; giving additional information

_____

_____

_____

_____

Summarizing—pulling together ideas; restating suggestions clarifying progress

_____

_____

_____

_____

Understanding Worksheet—Exercise No. 5
Understanding behaviors that help maintain the cohesion of the team

Instructions: Think back to the activity you and your team just completed. Write quotes and specific examples that show how you and your teammates displayed the following kinds of behaviors.

Harmonizing—reducing tension; getting people to explore difficulties; mediating

_____

_____

Gate keeping—asking for clarification; creating opportunities for others to participate

_____

_____

Encouraging—being friendly, warm, and responsive; celebrating successes; validating another's point; using nondestructive humor

_____

_____

Compromising—modifying your thinking or position

_____

_____

Standard setting and testing—testing whether the group is satisfied with its process; pointing out ground rules when broken

_____

_____

Consensus testing—checking cohesion or readiness to come to a decision; sending up trial balloons; making sure all members are on board with a decision

_____

_____

Understanding Worksheet—Exercise No. 5
Understanding self behaviors

Instructions: Think back to the activity you and your team just completed. Write quotes and specific examples that show how you and your teammates displayed the following kinds of behaviors.

Interrupting—all talk at once; cutting people off

_____

_____

_____

Taking a position and defending it—"yes, but;" giving the same idea several times

_____

_____

_____

Judging ideas of others—"we already tried that;" put-downs; ridicule; ignoring

_____

_____

_____

Humor/sarcasm at someone's expense—"Oh, sure. You always say those dumb things."

_____

_____

_____

Giving excessive information/ideas/suggestions/opinions—war stories; side trips; dominating

_____

_____

_____

UNDERSTANDING EXERCISE NO. 6
Consensus Decision Making

Workout Plan

When to use
When the team wishes to explore how members' individual behaviors impact the team, or the team's usual, natural way to solve problems together.

Time
60 minutes

Materials
Team Consensus worksheet for each participant

Purpose/objectives

- Experience the differences in individual and team decision making.

- Increase understanding of what it takes for teams to achieve consensus.

- Experience the effectiveness of team decisions over individual decisions.

Grouping
Teams no larger than eight to 10 members. If your team is larger than this, work in groups.

Warm-up
Clarify "What is consensus?" Get definitions from the group. Summarize with the following two guidelines:

1. All have an opportunity to give their point of view and be heard by the group.

2. All are willing to live with and support the decision even if it is not the one they would have picked individually.

Review the consensus information sheets.

Aerobics:

1. Ask participants to start by reading the instructions. Allow 10 minutes for them to read and score their own responses.

2. Group meets for 30 minutes to come to consensus as a team.

3. Once you call time, disclose the correct ratings. Have them score the activity and compare individual with team scores on a flip chart. Key point: team ordinarily scores better than collection of individuals. You may find one or two people who score better than the team, but the overall team score will be superior to the individual scores on average.

Cooldown
Debrief: Have the team discuss what it did well and did not do well. It may start by rating how satisfied it was with (1) the answers the team came up with (product), and (2) the way the team worked together (process).

The team may set one or two improvement goals for how to work together more effectively.

NOTE
Best value comes from this exercise when you combine it with the analysis of task, maintenance, and self behaviors (Understanding Exercise No. 5).

You can purchase excellent consensus exercises that come with complete directions, scoring sheets, videos, and so forth. "Subarctic Survival," "Desert Survival," and several more are available.

UNDERSTANDING INFORMATION SHEET— EXERCISE NO. 6

Consensus decision making

What is consensus?
Consensus is not the same as 100 percent agreement. In consensus, team members determine that they actively support the decision of the team, even though it might not be their personal choice.

How do you know you are there?
When each member can say with confidence

1. "My personal views and ideas have been really listened to and considered."

2. "I have openly listened to and considered the ideas and views of every other team member."

3. "Whether or not this decision would have been my choice, I can support it and work toward its implementation."

Tips for reaching consensus

What to watch for

- Do not employ win/lose techniques such as voting or negotiating favors back and forth.

- Look to alternatives that are next most acceptable as ways to break a stalemate.

- Don't encourage members to give in to keep harmony.

Team Consensus Worksheet—Exercise No. 6

The following list consists of nine potential causes of death. Your task is to rank order this list from highest to lowest probability for an average American over the next 50 years (1 = highest probability of death, nine = lowest probability). After you have ranked these nine causes, you will meet with your teammates to develop a consensus ranking.

Causes	Step 1 Your individual ranking	Step 2 The team's ranking	Step 3 The expert ranking	Step 4 Difference between steps 1 & 3	Step 5 Difference between steps 2 & 3
Electrocution					
Fireworks					
Homicide					
Auto accident					
Botulism					
Tornadoes					
Firearms accident					
Airplane crash					
Asteroid impact					

Your Score _____   **Team Score** _____

UNDERSTANDING INFORMATION SHEET —EXERCISE NO. 6

Risk probabilities

Expert rankings*

Botulism	1	in	2,000,000
Fireworks	1	in	1,000,000
Tornadoes	1	in	50,000
Airplane crash	1	in	20,000
Asteroid impact	1	in	6,000
Electrocution	1	in	5,000
Firearms accident	1	in	2,000
Homicide	1	in	300
Auto accident	1	in	100

*Source: Clark R. Chapman, Ph.D., and David Morrison, Ph.D., reported in the *New York Times*, June 20, 1991.

UNDERSTANDING EXERCISE NO. 7
What Sport?

Workout Plan

When to use
To clarify independence/interdependence needs and issues.

Time
60 minutes

Materials
Three flip charts—one for each group, what sport information sheet

Purpose/objectives

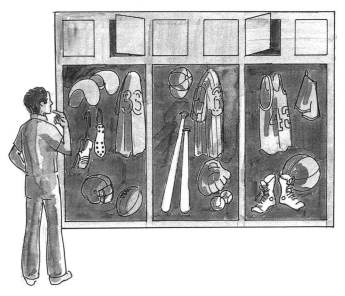

What sport?

- Use the metaphor of sports to help determine ways the team can organize itself to operate effectively.

- Determine the kind of coaching (and from whom) that is most effective for the way the team operates.

Grouping
Divide into three groups—one to focus on each of three sports (baseball, football, and basketball).

Warm-up
Ask, "What makes a team different from a work group?" (Looking for ideas like common goals and interdependence.) Read the What Sport? information sheet.

Aerobics

1. Assign each group the following questions:

   a. Think about the kind of work your team does. What can we learn from this sport?

b. When would it be advantageous for us as a team to act like a _____ team? How might that be different from the way we behave today?

c. When you are operating in that mode, what kind of coaching do you need?

2. Allow 30 minutes for each group to discuss and flip chart their ideas.

Cooldown
Give each team five minutes to share out its thinking. Summarize into key learnings for the team as a whole.

UNDERSTANDING INFORMATION SHEET—
EXERCISE NO. 7

What sport?

There are lessons to be learned from sports which apply to business and particularly to teams. Each of three major U.S. sports has something to teach us, about how to work most effectively in teamwork.

Consider how the following questions apply to your team.

- How are we interdependent?

- How closely do we work together?

- What is the basic work unit—an individual? Some grouping?

- How do we coordinate with each other?

- What kind of coach do we need?

- How do we get better?

Baseball*
In baseball, each person contributes to the game and the results (runs, outs, and so on) are pooled for a total team score. Interaction among members usually is limited to two or three players at a time.

Players are widely dispersed on the field. The basic unit in baseball is the individual. The basic tool to improve the team is improvement of individual competency, frequently through hiring new players.

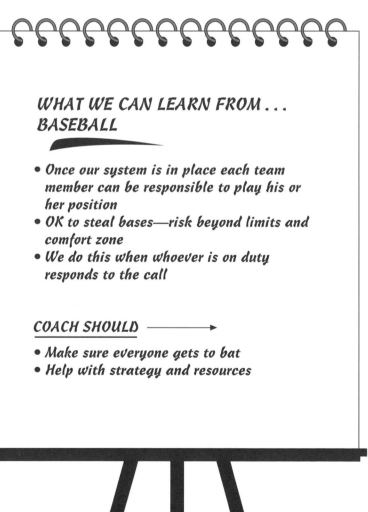

WHAT WE CAN LEARN FROM . . . BASEBALL

- Once our system is in place each team member can be responsible to play his or her position
- OK to steal bases—risk beyond limits and comfort zone
- We do this when whoever is on duty responds to the call

COACH SHOULD ⟶

- Make sure everyone gets to bat
- Help with strategy and resources

*Adapted from Robert W. Keidel, "Baseball, Football, and Basketball: Models for Business," *Organizational Dynamics,* Winter 1984.

WHAT WE CAN LEARN FROM . . . FOOTBALL

- *Make a game plan and send in squads to do different parts*
- *Learn good responses to attack so we don't have to figure it out at the time*
- *Coordinate efforts so teammates succeed*

COACH SHOULD ⟶

- *Make clear the overall strategy*
- *Make it so that others can call the plays as well*
- *Lead the Monday morning quarterbacking*

Football

In football, players are tightly huddled together and every player on the field is involved in every play. The basic unit is a large group or platoon (offense, defense, special teams). Overall performance is basically the unit's performance. If any player falters in the unit, the whole team can fail.

Improvement comes from developing individual and group competency.

Basketball

In basketball, the ball passes back and forth from one player to another. Although individuals shoot and score, the individual cannot win the game without the whole team. Every player is (1) involved in offense, defense, and transition, (2) handles the ball, and (3) attempts to score.

The basic unit in basketball is the whole team. Improvement comes from developing individual and team competency.

What are the implications of these sports analogies to your team?

What are the implications for leadership and coaching?

The coach's role in baseball has been described as tactical, with decisions made in real time. The coach determines the lineup, when to make substitutions, when to walk an opponent, use of pinch hitters, and so forth.

The coach's role in football is strategic. The team studies the opponents and practices to combat the opponent's strengths. Instructions for each play are precise and job descriptions are narrow.

The coach's role in basketball is integrative. The team must develop the ability to adjust and react. Cooperation and the ability to use each other's strengths are critical to the success of the team.

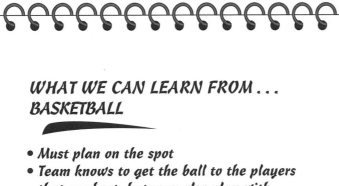

WHAT WE CAN LEARN FROM...
BASKETBALL

- *Must plan on the spot*
- *Team knows to get the ball to the players that are best, but may also play with whoever is on the spot—took the call*
- *Be flexible—get resources from anywhere*

COACH SHOULD →

- *Be clear about vision long term—what this game means short term—what it will take*
- *Share info with entire team, not individuals*

UNDERSTANDING EXERCISE NO. 8
Ten-Minute Team Process

Workout Plan

When to use
Once a week or regularly as decided. Plan to use as a quickie stand-up meeting, a team huddle.*

Time
10 minutes

Materials
Paper and pencil to record summary

Purpose/objectives

- Align members to the purpose of the team.

- Refocus members to a particular task.

- Regenerate enthusiasm for a task.

Grouping
All team members

The team huddle.

Warm-up
Pass out the rules ahead of the meeting. Tell members the task before the meeting so they can be prepared.

Aerobics

1. Think about the purpose of the team.

2. Each person states how they are contributing to the purpose and what they can do differently to direct their efforts toward that purpose (1 minute per person—timed).

*Adapted from T. Isgar. *Ten Minute Team* (Boulder, Colo.: Seluera Press, 1989).

3. Discuss the statements that were made.

4. Allow two minutes for summarizing.

Cooldown

Debrief: Someone summarizes. The summary is amended and accepted, written down, and distributed to members and management, when appropriate.

The Huddle System

Short meetings of small groups can be used for many purposes. Fifteen minutes is all that is allowed for group decision making in huddles at Time and Space, an advertising agency in Aberdeen, South Dakota. Three people are in each huddle (sales, production, money, training, planning, marketing, service, and fun). Huddles can spend up to $100 on their own, more with approval.

P. McDonald, "The Huddle System," *Inc.,* October 1992, 25.

UNDERSTANDING INFORMATION SHEET —EXERCISE NO. 8

Guidelines for the 10-minute team process

1. Each team member knows the ten-minute team task before the meeting.

2. Each team member is prepared.

3. Each team member makes a contribution.

4. The leader comments last.

5. Discussion occurs after everyone has made individual contributions.

6. Someone summarizes. The summary is amended and accepted.

7. Summary is written down and distributed to members and others when appropriate.

Other possible tasks for the 10-minute team process

1. Overall purpose of the team.

2. Progress against a particular goal.

3. Providing encouragement and support to others.

4. Customer contact.

UNDERSTANDING EXERCISE NO. 9
Process Check

Workout Plan

When to use
At the end of any team meeting

Time
10 minutes

Materials
Flip chart, colored markers, copy of team ground rules or operating agreements

Purpose/objectives

- Focus team's attention on how they work together as well as what they accomplish.

- Create an atmosphere of candidness without blame.

- Build a habit of continuous improvement in team's behavior as they work together.

Grouping
All team members

Process check.

Warm-up
At the end of the meeting, the team turns to the ground rules set or the operating agreements in place. Someone suggests one or two of them as the focus of the process check.

Examples: Stay with the times set on the agenda.

Listen without interrupting.

Aerobics

1. Each team member silently rates the agreement or ground rule on a scale of 1 to 10, according to the performance of the team in that particular meeting.

1 is the lowest rating. For listening, for example, this might mean that many interruptions occurred, or it might mean that everyone talked at once.

10 is the highest rating. For listening, this would indicate that people really focused on each others' ideas and gave each person time to share their real thinking with the team.

5 is an average rating. For listening, this shows that some listening is occurring, and that in some cases the team did not listen as agreed.

Ratings can fall anywhere on the 1 to 10 scale.

2. After all members have done their ratings silently, they are collected on the flip chart and displayed on a continuum.

1	2	3	4	5	6	7	8	9	10
	x	x		x	x	x		x	x
		x			x	x			
					x				

3. When the ratings are all displayed, those who rated *listening* high (9 and 10) are asked to share their thinking, their reason for rating that way. All others listen without commenting or arguing their own thinking.

4. Those who rated *listening* low (2 and 3) are then asked to share their thinking. Again, all members listen to the differing perceptions without commenting.

Cooldown
The team either sets a goal for continuous improvement for the next meeting, or determines that no goal needs to be set based on what was said.

NOTE
Repeat this process check on the same dimension at the next meeting, or for several meetings to ensure that improvements occur.

UNDERSTANDING EXERCISE NO. 10
Box and Bubble

Workout Plan

When to use
As a check or assessment of the team's balance between concrete, detailed, practical approaches and creative, big picture, innovative approaches.*

Time
1 hour

Materials
Box and Bubble worksheet for each team member, one transparency of Box and Bubble worksheet, overhead projector

Purpose/objectives

- Help the team work both in practical and creative ways to maximize effectiveness.

- Minimize the natural tension about how to approach the team's work.

Grouping
All team members

Warm-up
Introduce the idea or refer back to the idea that the box represents all the team's concrete, detailed, structured, left-brained, hard activities and approaches. The bubble represents the intuitive, creative, unstructured, right-brained, soft activities and approaches. Although both are valuable and useful, many teams tend to overuse one or use the wrong one (the one the team prefers). This creates gaps in team thinking and also communication problems with key constituents who are not working in the same mode.

*The concept of box and bubble comes from David K. Hurst, "Of Boxes and Bubbles and Effective Management," *Harvard Business Review,* May/June 1984, 78.

Aerobics

1. On the box and bubble worksheet, team members rate their perceptions of how they see *present approaches to their work,* using an X to mark along the continuum shown.

2. Each also marks with an O where he or she believes the *most effective approaches to his or her work* would be.

3. Each member's marks are transferred to the overhead transparency version of the worksheet.

4. Together, team members discuss the areas where there is a wide range of markings, listening to each person's perception and thinking, without arguing or disagreeing.

Cooldown

After all items have been discussed, the team determines one or two goals to put into place for improved effectiveness.

NOTE

If the team repeats this activity periodically, similarly to a process check, the goals can be short-term focuses—each time adding to effectiveness by focusing on a particular area.

Understanding Worksheet—Exercise No. 10
Box and bubble

Rate each dimension.
- X = Where our focus is now
- O = Where we need to be for maximum effectiveness

BOX	BUBBLE
Science **Hard/Rational**	**Art** **Soft/Intuitive**

Task Focus	People Focus
Controlled My focus	Inclusive Our mission
Planned	Spontaneous
Manage	Influence
Produce	Create
Content	Process

The concept of the box and bubble comes from:
Hurst, David K. Hurst, "Of Boxes and Bubbles and Effective Management," *Harvard Business Review,* May/June 1984, 78.

UNDERSTANDING EXERCISE NO. 11
Leadership Transition Meeting

Workout Plan

A new CEO took over an existing company. After about eight months, he decided to hold a leadership transition meeting with his direct reports. As dialogue moved forward, the room remained quiet and attentive, but he could sense a tension within the room. When they got to the question, "How would you describe the future of this team?", the new CEO told them he was very pleased with their work. He painted a picture of their future together.

Team members were astonished. All had assumed the new CEO would want to bring in his own senior management team and they would be fired. With this moment behind them, the new CEO and team were ready to move forward together.

When to use
When an existing team has a new leader. This exercise also can be used when there is a need to clarify expectations between group members and the leader.

Time
2 to 4 hours

Materials
Flip chart paper, marking pens, masking tape, transition questions

Purpose/objectives

- To accelerate the process by which individual team members and the new leader coordinate their understanding of each other and become more efficient and effective

Grouping
All team members

Warm-up
Explain that the goal for the session is to get a better understanding of the new leader and his/her preferred ways of working with the team, and to give the leader a better understanding of the team, its mission, and work situation.

Aerobics

1. Pass out the team members' worksheet.

2. Divide the team into smaller groups if there are more than five people.

3. Assign groups to discuss the questions and write down a consensus of their answers on flip chart paper. The team leader does the same thing alone.

4. The groups select a spokesperson to report to the rest of the team and the leader.

5. Allow 30 minutes to an hour to formulate the answers.

6. The team leader answers the leader's questions first. As the answers are given, encourage questions and elaboration.

7. Each team group reports to the leader and the rest of the group, one question at a time, round robin. The facilitator should ask members to look for areas of agreement and post these. Where there are differences of opinion, ask, "How can we work together, given these differences? Are there compromises that will make each other more comfortable?"*

Cooldown
These agreements can become the temporary operating agreements for the team. As time passes, they may need to be revisited and modified.

---

*More questions can be found in F. Petrock, "Just Tell Us What It Is You Want," *Business Month*, December 1989, 86.

UNDERSTANDING INFORMATION SHEET— EXERCISE NO. 11

Transition meeting questions for team leader

Select those that are relevant to your team and add any of your own.

1. Describe your role in the group as you see it.
   What previous experience do you feel will be of particular value in meeting the demands of this role?

2. How would you describe the mission of this team/organization?

3. How would you describe the future of this corporation/team/organization?

4. What do you consider to be the three biggest challenges you face as the team leader?

5. What is your leadership philosophy?
   What motivates people? Why do people work?
   How would you or previous subordinates describe your operating/management style?

6. What would be an ideal employee/team member/direct report in your eyes?

7. How do you like to be communicated with (face-to-face, by memo, and so on)?

8. What are your hot buttons, those things that really make you angry?

9. How would you like to see this team/management group operating together?

10. What concerns do/did you have taking over this new group?

11. What can group members do to be of help to you?

UNDERSTANDING INFORMATION SHEET— EXERCISE NO. 11

Transition meeting questions for team members

Select those that are relevant to your team and add any of your own.

1. What questions do you have about roles, accountabilities, and related expectations?

2. How would you describe the mission of this team/organization?

3. How would you describe the future of this corporation/team/ organization?

4. What do you consider to be the three biggest challenges the team/organization faces?

5. What is your leadership philosophy?

6. What is an ideal boss/team leader for you?
    What don't you like in a boss/team leader?

7. How do you like to be communicated with (in other words, face-to-face, by memo)? How do you like to receive recognition/ reprimands? Bad news?

8. What are hot buttons for you, those things that really make you angry?

9. How would you like to see this team/management group operate together?

10. What concerns do/did you have about the formation of this new management group/team?

11. What do you like best about the way this group has operated in the past?

12. What are some specifics you would like the leader to consider to help make the transition go well?

UNDERSTANDING EXERCISE NO. 12
Best Boss

Workout Plan

When to use
When the team leader wants feedback on effectiveness or a report card from team members, in order to improve leadership effectiveness within the team.

Time
30 to 60 minutes

Materials
Flip chart, colored markers

Purpose/objectives

- Allow the leader to understand the kinds of behaviors and actions the team believes would improve effectiveness of leadership for the team.

- Provide a structure for feedback that includes both positive reinforcement for effective leadership practices, and areas to focus on for growth.

- Create an atmosphere for open, supportive feedback.

Grouping
All team members and the leader. A team member should lead this activity so that the leader can be more reflective and able to listen.

Warm-up
Set the stage for openness by asking the team to be candid and to help build effective leadership by giving open feedback that is both positive and supportive of strengths, and that encourages growth and development.

Aerobics

1. Team members reflect and do a silent brainstorm on paper. Who was the most effective boss or leader with whom they have worked? In thinking of that leader, what was the characteristic about that person

that was so effective? How did the leader behave that played that characteristic out? What was the impact of that leader's behavior on team members?

2. Ideas are collected from each team member and listed on a flip chart.
Person   **Characteristic**   **Behavior**   **Impact**

3. For the present team leader's report card, all members are asked to rate the team leader by placing a (+) on two characteristics perceived as strengths and two areas where focus could help the team (–).

4. When all marks have been made on the flip chart, the leader and team examine the data and choose two areas of strength. Members give the leader examples of how those behaviors have helped achieve team effectiveness in specific situations. They then look at two areas of growth and team members make specific requests for support needed from the leader, and give examples of how that behavior would enable them to work more effectively.

FOR NEXT WEEK:

1. Every morning check in so all members have current info (Use voice mail!)

2. Supervisor "On-Call Schedule" posted to help find them

Cooldown
Team leader summarizes the feedback received, both strengths and requests, and makes one or two offers to the team of actions he/she will take to improve the leadership support given.

NOTE
It is a good idea for team leaders to plan for some way to receive feedback as they move forward, such as one-on-one meetings in a month, or repeating the report card in four months. Growth occurs best when there is follow-up to ensure focus on the changes determined, or when this is a frequent, ongoing feedback process.

UNDERSTANDING FACTOR NO. 3
The Organization

Definition: Understanding how to get things done within the larger organization and how your work supports the organization's mission.

About understanding the organization

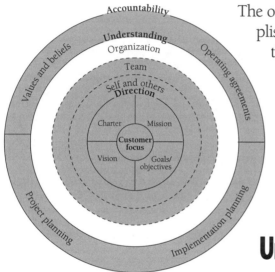

The organizational culture plays a role in enabling a team to accomplish its mission. What will the organization support? What are the taboos and informal rules for getting things done? Effective teamwork requires an understanding of how to work within this context for the good of your team.

Understanding the organization actions

Identify key stakeholders. Observe and audit the culture to position the team so it can effectively anticipate and influence the organization.

Understanding the organization questions

- What do we know that will allow us to work successfully in our organization's culture?

- How does our work fit into the larger purpose of the organization?

UNDERSTANDING EXERCISE NO. 13
Culture Audit

Workout Plan

Time
60 minutes

Materials
Culture audit worksheet for each team member; one overhead transparency of culture audit to collect the data for all to see visually

Purpose/objectives

- To focus team growth and development activities on the most necessary changes

- To honor and celebrate team strengths and successes

Grouping
Entire team

Warm-up
Each team member rates the team on each dimension shown on the worksheet. Ratings are for both where the team is today, and where the individual believes the team will need to be in coming years.

Aerobic

1. Team members record their ratings on an overhead slide or on a big chart on the wall that shows each dimension.

2. The team looks for both places where the team is now where it needs to be, and gaps that indicate growth needs. Planning is done based on how to close the gaps.

Cooldown

Note: It is important to end this exercise having identified only the two or three major actions or areas for focus. Too many can become demotivating and overwhelming for the team.

NOTE

This exercise can be repeated over time to determine progress or to identify where the team may be stuck.

Understanding Worksheet—Exercise No. 13
Culture audit

Please mark an X on the continuum where you believe we are as a team today. Mark an O where you believe we will need to be in coming years.

Fire fighting   Prevention
[——]

Reliance on a few favored resources   All employees as talent pool
[——]

Burn out people   Develop people
[——]

Individual rewards   Team rewards
[——]

Functional isolation   Cross-functional fluidity
[——]

One best way   Diversity
[——————————————————————————————————————]

Fear, skepticism   Trust, risk taking
[——————————————————————————————————————]

Bureaucratic   Simple
[——————————————————————————————————————]

Please the boss   Satisfy the customer
[——————————————————————————————————————]

Act when told   Act when needed
[——————————————————————————————————————]

Shoot the messenger   Open communication
[——————————————————————————————————————]

Power by title   Leadership by example
[——————————————————————————————————————]

UNDERSTANDING EXERCISE NO. 14
Culture Observation

Workout Plan

When to use
When the team is frustrated with getting things implemented, or wants to better understand the culture of the organization.

Time
1 to 2 hours

Materials
Culture observation worksheet, flip chart, marking pens

Purpose/objectives

- To observe the culture of the organization to gather information about how things are done

- To discuss the implications of these observations for the team

Grouping
All team members

Investigating your culture.

Warm-up
Give each person a culture observation worksheet. State that today's purpose is to study our own company as if we were outside observers. It might work to pretend that we are aliens or archaeologists who are observing the culture of our company. Later, we will discuss what the observations mean and what implications they have for our team.

Aerobics

1. Individuals go out to watch what is happening and write at least 10 observations from different parts of the organizations. This requires 15 to 30 minutes. They also can make notes on what they think these observations mean. They also draw conclusions about the meaning of what they have seen.

2. When they return, working in groups of five or so, team members discuss the observations and inferences. This takes another 30 minutes.

Write these instructions for their discussion on a flip chart:

1. Kinds of things observed, by category.

2. Examples of same and different inferences from same observations.

3. Problems encountered (interference) from knowing too much about the culture.

4. What inferences can you make about this culture based on your own observations?

5. What are the implications for the team?

Cooldown

Assemble all the group together again. Ask for each group to report and discuss each question, one at a time. List the implications and ask if people agree. Decide together whether the team needs to take particular actions based on what they learned.

Understanding Worksheet—Exercise No. 14

Cultural observation worksheet

Observation	Inference	Implications
1.		
2.		
3.		
4.		
5.		
6.		
7.		
8.		
9.		
10.		

Fitness Area IV: Accountability Exercises

Definition: Accountability within the team clarifies both who does what and how members will work together.

Accountability beyond the team clarifies what commitments the team has made for getting results, who else needs to be informed or consulted, where to get resources, and how to keep key stakeholders involved and committed.

About accountability

Internally, work on accountability is focused on how the team will work together. Who is responsible for what? How and when will meetings be run? All considerations that could get in the way of team cohesiveness are examined and discussed. Members come to consensus on how to operate and on the consequences for breaking agreements.

External to the team itself, fit teams are aware of others who are involved in and affected by their work. They don't let things fall through the cracks or face political pressure because they didn't communicate with key people who are involved or affected. They are clear about who to involve in every aspect of their work.

For a special project team, the project plan is the ultimate vehicle for tracking the team's progress. After goals and objectives are laid out, the project plan becomes the evaluation roadmap.

Accountability actions

To clarify member-working relationships, teams develop statements of beliefs and values and operating agreements. Accountability activities for project planning include developing matrixes of key tasks and defining member roles for those tasks, or using project-planning techniques such as Gantt charts, Pert charts, and so forth. In implementation planning, key stakeholders are identified, as well as their needs, level of involvement, and strategies for obtaining and keeping their commitment and support.

Accountability *inside* the team questions

- How and when will meetings be run?

- Who is responsible for what?

- How will conflicts be resolved?

- What behaviors are encouraged or taboo on the team?

- When will consensus decision making be appropriate, and when not?

- How will we support team decisions when we are not particularly excited about them?

Accountability *outside* the team questions

- Who will initiate key tasks?

- Who needs to be informed or consulted?

- Who holds veto power?

- Whose input and resources will be needed?

- How can we get the support and commitment of those who can make or break our success?

- How can we ensure consideration of factors that are most critical to our success?

Exercises in this section

- Accountability Factor No. 1: Values

    1. Values Statements

    2. If-Then-Then

- Accountability Factor No. 2: Operating Agreements

    3. Operating Agreements

    4. Negotiating Ground Rules

    5. Individual Contracting

- Accountability Factor No. 3: Project Planning

    6. Team Responsibility Chart

    7. ABC Priorities

- Accountability Factor No. 4: Implementation Planning

    8. Implementation Responsibility Chart

    9. Stakeholder Support

    10. Critical Success Factors

ACCOUNTABILITY FACTOR NO. 1
Values and Beliefs

Definition: Agreeing on the underlying principles of what is important to the team and organization and what drives decisions and ways of operating.

About values and beliefs

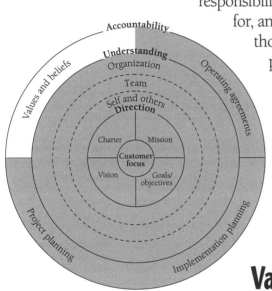

Values and beliefs are the broadest form of accountability. The team has the responsibility to know what it stands for, and what its organization stands for, and then to choose actions that support and are in alignment with those values. How is daily work impacted if the team wants to be a partner to its customers, or believes it needs to be highly flexible? What does it mean to do work with integrity?

Values and beliefs actions

Expressly stating values and beliefs for the team helps each member stay in alignment not only with the tasks and work, but with the more subtle aspects of how the work is done. Discussion about values ensures critical thinking on difficult issues and builds an atmosphere of open, candid communication.

Values and beliefs questions

- What are the values we want our team to live by?

- Which of our actions or behaviors support our values and which ones are in conflict?

- How would we like to be seen and known?

- How can we create an open atmosphere where together we can learn how to work consistently with our organization and team values?

VISION
We will position ourselves so when anyone thinks of borrowing money, needs business services, or wants ideas, they will automatically turn to us.

VALUES
We are

- *Customer-oriented*
- *Service-minded*
- *Efficient*
- *Knowledgeable*
- *Community-minded*

ACCOUNTABILITY EXERCISE NO. 1
Values Statements

Workout Plan

When to use
To clarify the underlying beliefs that drive team actions.

Time
2 to 4 hours

Materials
Values statement information sheet, flip chart, marking pens, masking tape

Purpose/objectives

- To create a statement of values that reflects the highest thinking and feeling of the team

- To develop a set of beliefs that will guide team members in daily decisions

Grouping
All team members

Values drive behaviors.

Warm-up
Introduce the topic by saying something like, "We all operate out of a set of values in our personal life and our work life. Since we spend so much of our life at work and with each other, it is reasonable that our work life should reflect our shared organization and team values."

Aerobics

1. Create a list of values by brainstorming.

2. Look at some of the areas on the values statement information sheet to stimulate thinking and add to the brainstormed list.

3. After there is agreement on the various values, divide the team into groups and ask the groups to each take flip chart paper and write a statement that they think is reflective of the team's thinking for each value.

4. Bring the statements together. Discuss. Come to consensus on one statement.

Cooldown

Brainstorm various dilemmas that the team may face and check the values statements to determine if they can help in guiding decisions and actions. How can we use the statement of values to help clarify gray areas in decision making in the daily work of the team? Decide how these value statements will be recorded and kept in a place for easy reference.

COMPANY EMPLOYEE CREED

I believe that if I am open and honest with my customers, I will earn their trust and I will feel good about myself.

I believe that with a positive and enthusiastic attitude, the customers will respond positively and my self-image and our company will achieve good results.

I believe that our products will enhance my customer's business.

I know that our business cannot survive without repeat customers.

I know that 80 percent of our business comes from 20 percent of our customers.

I believe that if I know, understand, and care about my customers' businesses, I can clarify their needs and help them to get what they want.

Southwest Airlines Values Fun.

One of the most successful airlines in the world is Southwest Airlines. The organizational culture derives from the following three core values:

"Value 1. Work should be fun . . . it can be play . . . enjoy it.

Value 2. Work is important . . . don't spoil it with seriousness.

Value 3. People are important . . . each one makes a difference."

A sense of humor and caring are criteria for employment.

> J. Quick, "Crafting Organizational Culture: Herb's Hand at Southwest Airlines," *Organizational Dynamics,* Winter 1993, 45–56.

Statement of Values

We strive to provide the highest level of service and base our actions on these values.

- We value our customers as our number-one priority.

- We listen to our customers' needs and concerns, understand their business, and look out for their interests.

- We strive for maximum efficiency and effectiveness.

- We provide added value in everything we do—or we don't do it.

- We maintain high standards of excellence, integrity, and quality.

- We value our employees and reward excellence and productivity.

- We practice teamwork within the organization and with our clients and recognize the unique and valuable contribution each member makes to the team.

Example of one team's values.

ACCOUNTABILITY INFORMATION SHEET—EXERCISE NO. 1

Values statements

Here is a partial list of areas where the team may wish to develop a standard of values or beliefs.

1. How do we treat our customers?

2. How do we treat each other?

3. How are mistakes handled?

4. How do we deal with others who fail to live up to their agreements?

5. What do we do when some of us are under tight deadlines and pressure?

6. How do we provide meaning and dignity to the workplace?

7. How do we recognize good work?

8. What do we want to be known for in the quality of our work?

9. What promises will we make to our customers?

10. What promises will we make to our employees?

ACCOUNTABILITY EXERCISE NO. 2
If–Then–Then

Workout Plan

Values Drive Business

We know a team from the international department of a large financial company who defined specific key indicators of actions that either support or detract from the values and philosophy. Because the company values customer responsiveness, the international department commits to and tracks one-day turnaround for applications and assistance with all import/export bills of lading. As a result, their department's business has doubled each year for the past three years.

When to use
To spell out what values look like in different scenarios and what kinds of behaviors will be in evidence when the values are being considered. You may wish to use the values generated in Accountability Exercise No. 1 as a basis for this exercise or start from scratch.

Time
2 hours

Materials
Flip chart, colored markers

Purpose/objectives

- To help team members see how the values of the team help determine daily actions and activities

- To clarify acceptable and unacceptable behaviors

- To act as a guide for daily decisions in unclear areas

Grouping
All team members

Warm-up
Explain that the values usually describe how we wish to be seen by the customer and help establish the boundaries between what is good and acceptable to do and what the team would reject or not respect. We need to get clear about our team's values and specific about how they apply to the team's work. This will help ensure that behaviors are appropriate as tasks are being accomplished.

First we will look at the values upon which we agree. Then we will talk about our strategy in making those values active. We also will discuss what it would look like to work from those values.

Aerobics

1. Team members brainstorm the values each would like the team to hold.

2. After the list is complete, each team member marks five values they see as particularly important. The top three or four are adopted as shared values—those that are most common and agreed upon by team members.

3. Each of the shared values is examined, using the following format to guide the analysis:

If we desire to work with	**Then** our strategy is	**Then** our behavior looks like
Honesty	Don't fudge when communicating with the customer	Real delivery dates
	Provide direct feedback of results and impact on each other	No gossiping Facts and data given Work through glitches together Surface potential problems as quickly as possible
	Leadership makes decisions from complete information	Bad news and good news both given Messengers not shot

Both value statements and behavior descriptions should be agreed to by consensus of the team.

Cooldown

The strategies and descriptions become agreements the team has put in place. They provide a basis for discussion to determine how to handle gray areas and conflicts.

ACCOUNTABILITY FACTOR NO. 2
Operating Agreements

Definition: Making explicit agreements about the ways the team will work together to accomplish its goals.

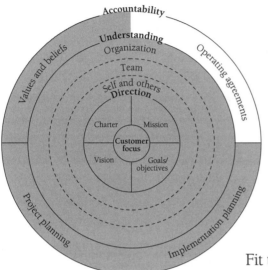

About operating agreements

Operating agreements serve two purposes for the team. They proactively define for team members the expectations between team members, and they provide a positive basis to work from when there is tension or difficulty among team members. Teams that spell out agreements up front are less likely to waste valuable time and energy on differences and disagreements.

Operating agreements actions

Fit teams define commitments. Operating agreements are in existence over a long period of time and are only changed or amended as needed. Teams also often set ground rules for a particular meeting or situation that are for that situation only and are not carried over into other kinds of work.

Operating agreements save wasted energy.

Operating agreements questions

- What do my team members expect from me and what can I expect from them?

- What will be OK and accepted in this team and what will not be allowed or acceptable?

- How do we need to work together for this particular situation in a way that will be most productive and advantageous?

ACCOUNTABILITY EXERCISE NO. 3
Operating Agreements

Workout Plan

When to use
This is particularly useful when a team is just starting as a way to generate good ideas. It also can serve as a conflict prevention measure.

Time
2 hours

Materials
Accountability Information Sheet for Exercise No. 3

Purpose/objectives

- To specify procedures and behaviors that the team agrees to use or to not use in their work together

- To make a contract between team members on issues critical to the team's effectiveness

- To form agreements that give people permission and the responsibility to talk about and work through the typical difficult times of working together, so issues are resolved before major problems or loss of productivity result

Grouping
All group members must be present for this activity so that agreements are developed and agreed to by everyone.

Team members support each other.

Warm-up
Ask team members to talk about some of the negative experiences they have had in previous teams, and why working on those teams was not satisfying. Have them focus on how team members worked together in those situations.

State that the goal of this activity is to ensure that this team does not repeat those mistakes or continue the bad habits that got in the way. Instead, we want to create an open relationship of support and candor.

Aerobics

1. In small groups, team members brainstorm and agree on one or two operating agreements to propose to the team. Each proposal should state

   • The agreement, that is, "We will . . . ," or "We agree. . . ."

   • Descriptions of what it looks like when done right

   • A suggested way to handle times when the agreement is not followed

2. Each proposal should be posted on a separate sheet of flip chart paper. Spend a few minutes allowing all team members to walk around and study the posted proposals.
3. Take the proposals one at a time and work for consensus on each part. First, consider the agreement, then what it looks like, then how to handle the times when team members slip.

Cooldown

Each team member should get the finalized agreements in written form. (Some teams agree to keep them in an obvious place; in other words, posted beside their desks, on a card for each to place beside them in staff meetings, on the pull-out board at their desk—wherever it will be a reminder, and available to be referred to as an aid to communicating in the difficult moments.)

NOTE

Operating agreements are most effective when each has been given thorough consideration by every team member and each has true buy-in. You are better off to get two good ones that everyone lives by, than 10 that are ignored. Some teams work on one at each meeting until they get several in place, rather than doing them all at one time.

Operating Agreements

- We agree to make sure all team members can give their ideas and that their ideas will be truly heard and considered by the team.

- Looks like:
  —Be an active listener (shown by paraphrasing, focusing, asking questions, summarizing and restating).
  —Be willing to listen to the opinions of others. (Be receptive, flexible, willing to compromise, ask for clarification.)
  —Keep an objective viewpoint. (Focus on the mission and values. Be aware of your own agenda and prejudices and try to stay open to the ideas of others.)
  —If you see ideas being put down or skipped over, stop the team by pointing out what you saw and allowing the idea to be given again.

- When this does not work, help each other by giving candid feedback and reminding your team partner of the agreement made.
  —"When you said 'No way!' it cut me off and made me feel you don't want to hear my thinking. Our agreement is to try to get all ideas on the table before making team decisions."

Example of one team's operating agreement.

ACCOUNTABILITY INFORMATION SHEET— EXERCISE NO. 3

Operating agreements

Ideas for topics

- Making key decisions—When will consensus be best? If not team consensus, how are other key decisions to be handled and what is the rationale? Who decides who decides?

- Running meetings—What techniques will be standard for the team (agenda, time allotments, regular breaks, starting and stopping on time, use of process checks)?

- Follow through on commitments—What can team members expect from one another on deliverables assigned from teamwork? When push comes to shove on priorities, how will conflicts be handled?

- Behavior norms—What is OK to do on this team, and what is not appreciated or accepted by team members?

- Delivering bad news—How can feedback be given when things go wrong? What is a team member's responsibility for sharing or withholding information that impacts team performance? How can tough news be given in a supportive way?

- Conflicts between team members—Who should initiate a discussion pertaining to a perceived conflict? When? What about involving others who were not part of a conflict? When should assistance be requested?

- Celebrating successes—What warrants a celebration? What kinds of celebrations make team members feel rewarded and valued?

- Roles and responsibilities—What are the expectations for the leader and for team members? Will we use a facilitator or timekeeper? Who will lead agenda items in meetings?

ACCOUNTABILITY EXERCISE NO. 4
Negotiating Ground Rules

Workout Plan

When to use
When you have a special meeting with your team or another group. When the group is not used to working together. When the team is working on a special project and you want to define how you are going to work together on that project.

Time
15 to 20 minutes

Materials
Flip charts and marking pens

Purpose/objectives

- To define the rules for how to work together

- To provide a reminder when we don't live up to the rules we have made

Grouping
All the members who are involved in a particular meeting or project

Warm-up
Remind the team that ground rules provide safety for being candid, help us police ourselves in sticking to the subject, and define courtesy and expectations for each person.

Ground rules.

Aerobics

1. Brainstorm a list of ideas of ground rules that team members see as particularly helpful to the work being addressed in the session. Some areas that may be helpful to agree on are

Physical comfort—breaks, standing up, getting drinks and food
Use of time—promptness from breaks, time limits on agenda topics, air time per person per topic
Rights—to disagree constructively, confidentiality
Respect for each other—put-downs, the value of each person's idea
Roles—the leader, the facilitator, outsiders, members

2. List the ground rules that have been developed. Ask for discussion, agreement, disagreement.

3. Come to agreement on several areas. Record them and hang them on the wall. Ask each person to refer to them when necessary.

Cooldown
Use the ground rules to help stay on track. Members can refer back to agreements made and not attack the personal behaviors of another. At the end of the meeting, return to the ground rules and ask for comments on how well the group lived up to its agreements.

— GROUND RULES —
(from a team with a sense of humor)

1. *No broken arms*
2. *Be as open in discussion as you can comfortably be*
3. *Be candid and direct*
4. *Focus on problems and solutions, not on people*
5. *Accentuate the positive*
6. *Be punctual*
7. *Share imported beer!*
8. *Be creative, innovative in thinking*
9. *Everyone participates*

ACCOUNTABILITY EXERCISE NO. 5
Individual Contracting

Workout Plan

When to use

To provide feedback to each member of the team on a personal basis. Generally, there are more areas of agreement among team members than disagreements. This exercise can reinforce those areas of agreement and help members deal with minor disagreements among team members. There may be some members who are uncomfortable confronting other, more dominant members of the team. Use this exercise when you simply want to improve the working relationships of the various team members.

Time

15 minutes for team meeting; 15 to 30 minutes per each individual contract

Materials

Contract worksheets

Individual contracting on expectations.

Purpose/objectives

- To promote better working relationships among team members

- To prevent conflicts before they begin or escalate

Grouping

All members of the team

Warm-up

Solicit from team members their opinion on how individual contracts could improve the effectiveness of the team. Remind them that this exercise is one where each will work with every other person on the team to reach agreements on how they want to work best with each other.

Aerobics

1. Pass out contract worksheets.

2. Explain that each member will meet with every other member to gain agreement on the questions on the worksheet. It will be the responsibility of each member to make time at lunch, breaks, or after work, to discuss their working relationships and agree on how they can work best together.

3. Walk through the contract worksheet and explain each idea and ask for questions.

4. Some people may wish to begin right away. Set a reasonable time to complete the contracting and meet back together and discuss the results.

Cooldown

At the follow-up meeting, debrief with the following questions:

1. What did you learn from this process?

2. What kinds of things did you hear that pleased you?

3. What kinds of things did you hear that surprised you?

4. What will you do differently as a result of this process?

5. How will this process make our team better?

Accountability Worksheet—Exercise No. 5
Individual contract

Each team member fills out one worksheet for every other team member. Members meet in pairs and discuss and agree upon contract.

Contract between _____   Date _____

and _____

1. What I want you to continue to do

_____

2. What I wish you would do more of

_____

3. What I wish you would do less of

_____

4. What I will do to better support you

_____

ACCOUNTABILITY FACTOR NO. 3
Project Planning

Definition: The planning methods used to ensure the right things are done, done right, and on time.

About project planning

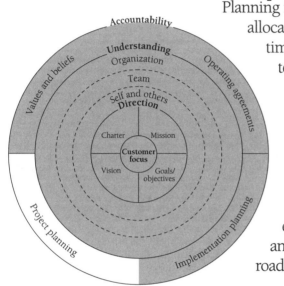

Planning for the team's output requires careful consideration of the allocation of resources. As teams set goals, they also need to define timelines and accountabilities. A frequent source of conflict for team members is in accountability for the team's output. Members often duplicate some efforts while other important items are neglected. People need to agree on who does what and with what support. There also must be agreement on the priorities of actions to achieve the goals.

Some special project teams need to recognize the interdependencies of project milestones (in other words, certain events must happen before others can proceed). After the goals and objectives are laid out, the project plan is the team's evaluation roadmap.

Project planning actions

Team members examine the total work of the team and the allocation of resources to assure that there are no overlaps or items that fall through the cracks. They develop action plans for specific step-by-step activities, and prioritization of those activities.

Project planning questions

- What roles do different team members play and how are those roles critical to our success as a team?

- Do we have a plan for projects with assignments, milestones, and deadlines?

- Who will support me in my responsibilities?

- What goals, projects, and activities will provide the biggest payoff for the team?

ACCOUNTABILITY EXERCISE NO. 6
Team Responsibility Chart

Workout Plan

When to use
During the planning and goal-setting process. New teams will find this exercise essential. Intact work teams can benefit by looking at everyone's role as responsibilities and priorities shift. This exercise can help prevent conflict by clarifying who on the team will do what.

Clarify leadership and support.

Time
1 hour

Materials
Flip chart paper, marking pens, Team Responsibility Chart

Purpose/objectives

- To create a visual matrix of team member responsibility for major team goals

- To clarify responsibilities

- To ensure all major goals are covered

Grouping
All members of the team

Warm-up
Build a matrix on flip chart paper like the one on the matrix worksheet. Across the top, list the major team goals. Down the left-hand side, list the names of each team member.

Aerobics

1. Discuss each goal and clarify.

2. Ask each team member to come forward and place an *R* for primary Responsibility for each goal, an *S* for Support, a *C* for Consult or provide advice, and an *I* for need to be Informed regarding the goal and progress.

3. Examine the matrix for gaps and overlaps. Ask

   - "Are there any goals where no one has the assigned responsibility?"

   - "Are there any goals where two or more people feel they have the major responsibility?"
     If yes to either question, "What are we going to do about it?"

   - "Does everyone have the support they need for their responsibilities?"

   - "Are there too many *I*s? Will we have to spend too much time keeping everyone informed?"

Cooldown
Copy the matrix for each team member so that it is easy for them to know who to go to as they progress in their daily work.

INSURANCE CLAIMS DEPARTMENT
TEAM RESPONSIBILITY CHART

		Answer customers	Track claims	Interpret disputes	Pay Claims
1.	**Donnie**	I		I	I
2.	**M.J.**	R	I		S
3.	**Dorothy**		R	S	R
4.	**Terry**	C		R	
5.	**Debbie**	R	I		S
6.	**Gloria**		S		

R = Primary responsibility
S = Support (active involvement)
I = Keep informed
C = Consult or provide advice

Example of a team responsibility chart.

Accountability Worksheet—Exercise No. 6
Team responsibility chart

Name of team member	Goal 1	Goal 2	Goal 3	Goal 4	Goal 5	Goal 6	Goal 7
1.							
2.							
3.							
4.							
5.							
6.							
7.							
8.							
9.							
10.							

R = Primary responsibility
S = Support (active involvement)
I = Keep informed
C = Consult or provide advice

ACCOUNTABILITY EXERCISE NO. 7
ABC Priorities

Workout Plan

When to use
At the launch of a major project or whenever there is an overload of tasks that need to be accomplished.

Time
1 to 3 hours, depending on the scope of tasks to be prioritized

Materials
Flip chart, colored markers, information about projects or goals

Purpose/objectives

- Categorize and clarify tasks and activities to be accomplished.

- Determine high-priority tasks and those that can be delegated or delayed.

Grouping
Can be done by a small group or entire team.

Warm-up
Brainstorm or list on the flip chart all the possible team tasks and activities without regard to scope, timeline, or level of detail.

Aerobics

1. Categorize each activity as *A, B,* or *C* according to level of priority.

2. Within each category, sequence activities on one list and prioritize on a second list.

3. From all lists, make a plan that includes
   Highest priority–short term
   Highest priority–long term
   To do ourselves
   To delegate

Cooldown

The short term list should extend over a short time period. For the first week or two for a typical project, one or two days if your overall timeline is very short. At the end of that time, repeat the process to establish a new list.

NOTE

The value of this exercise is in ordering tasks to relieve the pressure of all that seemingly needs to be done simultaneously.

ACCOUNTABILITY FACTOR NO. 4
Implementation Planning

Definition: The planning methods used to ensure that the work of the team will be accepted by the rest of the organization.

About implementation planning

The work of a team is not accomplished in a vacuum. Whether the team is at the top of the organization or somewhere in the middle, acceptance by others must be considered. Teams at the top must plan for the commitment of employees to their vision and goals. Teams in the middle must consider the team's stakeholders, sponsors, and customers. For any team, good team output without adequate implementation planning can lead to frustration and minimized results.

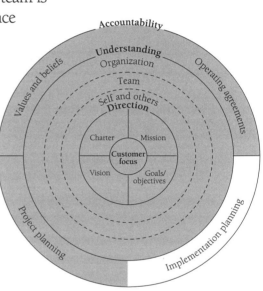

Implementation planning exercises

Exercises in this section include analysis of stakeholders, organization culture and social norms, communication needs, and, finally, examination of the critical success factors needed for implementation.

Implementation planning questions

- Who has a stake in our work? What do they need or want to know about what we are doing?

- How do we build commitment of others to the work of this team?

- What do we need from others to accomplish our goals? How will we get their help?

- How do we work within the cultural and social norms of this organization to accomplish our goals?

- What critical factors must be taken into account in planning for the success of our efforts?

ACCOUNTABILITY EXERCISE NO. 8
Implementation Responsibility Chart

Workout Plan

When to use
At the beginning of a project to make sure the right people beyond the team are informed. Use in the middle of a project to provide a check on changing processes and priorities. This chart helps the team make sure all key stakeholders are appropriately involved.

Time
2 hours

Materials
Charting worksheet, list of defined tasks for a key process

Purpose/objectives

- To clarify who has major responsibility for a specific aspect of a key process and the tasks to manage that process

- To get agreement on who else needs to be involved and why

- To ensure that critical stakeholders are involved appropriately

Grouping
All team members who have responsibility for a process

Warm-up
Fill out the charting worksheet by entering the list of tasks for the process down the left side. Across the top, add the names of key functions or individuals who play some part in the decision making or implementation of those tasks.

Aerobics

1. Work in pairs to propose the appropriate responsibility for each function or individual listed, on each task.

2. Pairs present their thinking to the entire group and get validation or modify according to the group's input. Continue this until each task has been completed.

Cooldown

Allow some time at the end to look at the big picture of the process and share key insights team members had from working through the activity.

Accountability Worksheet—Exercise No. 8
Implementation responsibility chart

Instructions: Assign a responsibility behavior to each of the objectives or major tasks for each function or individual as appropriate.

(R) = Person/function that initiates action to ensure that process/task is carried out. Owns the accountability.

(A) = Approval, or right to veto. This person MUST review and can approve or veto.

(S) = Support—provides information, resources, etc.

(I) = Inform—This person must be informed of the outcome, decision, action, but does not influence. Needs to understand rationale.

(P) = Provides input—has a need to give expertise, advice, or tailoring information.

List goals or objectives down the left side. List individuals or functions across the top.

1.						
2.						
3.						
4.						
5.						
6.						
7.						

ACCOUNTABILITY EXERCISE NO. 9
Stakeholder Support

Workout Plan

When to use
This is appropriate early in a new project, or with an intact workteam, when things are getting bogged down and you need to fall back, regroup, and think strategically.

Definition
Stakeholders are those people outside our team who have an interest or a stake in our work.

Time
1 hour

Materials
Flip chart, colored markers

Purpose/objectives

- Identify key stakeholders and determine strategies for gaining or keeping their commitment to the work of the team.

- Develop specific strategies for each key stakeholder for increased support.

Grouping
All team members or sometimes subgroups of the team who have a particular aspect of the project in mind

Warm-up
Have a quick open discussion about the people, departments, constituents who have input to, are impacted by, or need to implement the results of the work of the team. What could happen if the concerns and issues of those stakeholders are not considered?

Aerobics

1. Brainstorm a list of all stakeholders. Choose the top one-third.

2. For each key stakeholder, list what the team believes to be their top few concerns and issues.

3. Strategize how to demonstrate concern for each stakeholder's issues and how to plan for their needs and wants. Determine how to work with them to change perceptions, if those needs and wants are inconsistent with the direction of your work.

Cooldown

From the list of stakeholders, find one or two who are allowing your work to proceed, and strategize how to get them to become active champions. Find one or two who are either opposed, or apathetic, but their active support could be a big boost to your work. Strategize how to help them get on board.

STAKEHOLDER SUPPORT

X= Now
O=desired

Stakeholder	Oppose	Let happen	Help happen	Make happen
V.P. Sales Critical communication link to field			X............O	
OPS Manager Need daily decisions to be consistent with direction		X............O		
Finance $ Allocations are visible sign of commitment	X...............O			
CEO Active championing gives strong message to all of desired direction				X............O

ACCOUNTABILITY EXERCISE NO. 10
Critical Success Factors

Workout Plan

When to use
In the initial planning for a project work team.*

Time
2 hours

Materials
Flip chart, colored markers

Purpose/objectives

- Identify the factors that could make or break the success of the project.

- Focus actions on the most critical success factors to ensure that time
  and resources used on implementation are properly
  placed.

Grouping
All team members

Warm-up
Review the purpose of the project and its
strategies and goals. Remind team
members that no project lives in a
vacuum—many things beyond
the project work itself will
affect the project's
success or failure.

Critical success factors.

*Adapted from M. Hardaker and B. K. Ward, "Getting Things Done: How to Make a Team Work," *Harvard Business Review,* November–December 1987, 112–19.

Aerobics

1. Brainstorm a list of critical success factors—those factors beyond the work of the project that will ensure success or will become roadblocks that defeat the project.

2. Clarify each brainstormed factor and eliminate any redundancies on the list.

3. Prioritize the factors, listing from most critical to least critical. For the focus of this analysis, look at no more than the eight to 10 critical factors.

4. Review the project plan's tasks and activities. For each important project activity, identify which critical success factors must be taken into account.

5. Make a plan for actions to ensure that these factors are not overlooked as project activities are carried out.

Cooldown

Return to the project success factors farther into the project and use them as a process check. For each of the possible identified factors, ask team members to rate how well the team is managing actions to ensure that factor is incorporated into project activities and actions. Use this to refocus efforts as needed.

APPENDICES

Types of Teams

Teams can be classified on the basis of *duration, composition* of members, and *purpose.*

Duration can be

- Short

- Medium

- Ongoing

Composition can be

- Peers or vertically integrated

- Single department/division or cross-organizational boundaries

- Multi- or one-site representation

- Multidisciplinary

Purpose of teams can be to

- Perform the intact work team function

- Study and make recommendations

- Make something tangible happen

- Design and introduce major change

- Complete a project with a specific end date

Most companies have at least two types of teams in place.

1. Natural management teams—managers and their direct reports are very common.

2. Special teams, such as project teams, task forces, committees that are put together for a specific purpose.

Following are some examples of different kinds of teams and their characteristics.

Task forces—Generally there is no boss. Organized around one particular problem to solve or issue to work.

New product development—Usually cross-functional, interdepartmental, almost like a problem solving team. Must have commitment at every step or you will get sabotage.

Intact work teams—Most common, departmental.

Problem solving—Some task forces. Formed for a specific purpose, with an end time.

Quality improvement—May be cross-functional, intra- or inter-departmental. More ongoing, take on new problems as others are solved.

Start-up—Brand new team, often a new function, new members.

Transition—Can be for start-up or mergers, any movement in new direction or culture. Short term to deal with change.

Strategy setting—Generally a top management team or core team.

This list does not include all the kinds of teams that are found in today's enterprise. No matter what kind of team you are, the team fitness model will help you build a healthy productive working atmosphere.

New Team Start-Up

S tarting a new team is exciting. You can save yourself a great deal of time in the transition by creating a strong foundation for action. You are fortunate, too, because the team is fresh and has no bad habits to change.

You may want to spend one or two days on the exercises we recommend, or you may build the fitness process into your regular team routine. Short, steady work builds strength, energizes team members, and enhances endurance, and getting a kick start is helpful as long as you remember to keep on with regular work.

Where do you begin? You may choose an exercise from each of the four areas. A suggested sequence follows, but use your own situation and build what is right for your particular team.

1. You will want to get to know each other as quickly as possible. You can start with Understanding Exercise No. 1, In-depth Intros. Be sure to include this question, "Why do I think I was selected to be on this team?"

2. The scope and boundaries of the team's work must be defined. Direction Exercise No. 1, New Team Charter, helps accomplish this.

3. It is time to develop a mission statement to ensure everyone is aligned around a common purpose. Use Direction Exercise No. 6 or No. 7.

4. To further understand each other and your leader and how you will work together, you could do Understanding Exercise No. 11, Leadership Transition.

5. Now that you know more about your team members, you can define your customers and their expectations of your team. Customer Focus Exercise No. 1, Who is the Customer? and Customer Focus Exercise No. 5, What Do Our Customers Want and Expect from Us? are useful here.

6. You have a mission; you know your scope and boundaries. Use Direction Exercises to lay out your goals and objectives. If the goals come down through the organization to you, use Direction Exercise No. 8. If you are chartered to develop your own goals, use Direction Exercise No. 9.

7. Following your goal-setting process, you can develop a chart of major responsibilities for each of the goals so that you don't overlap each others' territory or things don't fall through the cracks. Use Accountability Exercise No. 6, Responsibility Charting. Or you may need to prioritize first with Accountability Exercise No. 7, ABC Priorities.

8. You've laid the groundwork for how you will work together, now it is useful to develop some simple and specific operating agreements between team members. Use Accountability Exercise No. 3, Operating Agreements.

9. Once you have had some time to work together and gather a few quick wins, you may move to implementation planning to make sure your work will be accepted in your organization. Use Accountability Exercise No. 9, Stakeholder Support.

10. Continue to select exercises that seem to fill a need. After your team has worked together for six to eight weeks, take the fitness meter and see how you're doing. We bet you will score high.

Good luck with your new team!

appendix c

How to Begin with an Existing Team

Some team leaders find it uncomfortable to begin a new team fitness program. They are not sure where to start. They have concerns such as "Will the other team members think the new emphasis implies that we're not a good team now?"

Here's a way you might begin.

1. Bring the group together for a 30-minute meeting to discuss your ideas. You might say something like the following:

   "I've been hearing people talk about teams and doing some reading about teams. Many teams seem to be getting more productive and creative. People are having more fun and getting better results on their teams.

   We work well together, but I think we could be even better. I have this new book which is based on a fitness model. Just as athletes continue to train in order to improve, just as we all strive to achieve a certain level of fitness, teams can work on their *team* fitness."

2. Show them this book and the fitness model. Explain each of the components and its importance.

3. Ask each person to fill out the fitness meter. Pass out copies of the meter. Assign someone to score them and bring the results back to the next meeting or do it together now.

4. Discuss the fitness meter results.

5. You could use "Are We a Team or a Work Group?" Understanding Exercise No. 4 to encourage people to talk about the way you are working together now.

6. End the meeting with plans for the next one. Ask team members what they think about this new emphasis. If there are concerns, record them on a flip chart.

   The answer to concerns at this point might be, "I don't know. I want to find out, too. I'm enthused about making a special effort to improve our team's fitness."

7. If your team has never done any work on team effectiveness in the past, you may need to take an active role and plan and lead in the beginning. If your team is experienced in team development, you may do the planning all together or a small group may plan and propose activities back to the rest. Wherever you begin, you can use the model to help guide your activities and to determine how to focus your team's efforts.

appendix d

Teams and Time

You may have been working on your team's fitness for some time by now, but it is not over. Stages in team development and the leader's role change as teams and circumstances change. One factor to understand in helping your team become fit is that team fitness is a moving target. Teams don't stay static over time, and you will be in some stage, or some reiteration of a stage most of the time. New members are added, goals change, members leave, new organizational directions come into play. When these things happen, you must fall back and regroup. Even if things are constant, the relationships of team members will change over time, and the team will need to continue to work to stay in shape. We all know what happens when you quit your exercise program for three months. It is much the same with your team. Getting fit and staying fit is not a one-time event, but rather a commitment to ongoing attention and work to make certain the team can function at its optimum.

In the early stages, when you are starting up your team, you may need to be quite directive and lay out a plan for how the team gets its fitness activities accomplished. During this time team members may be enthusiastic about outcomes of the work to come, but may also be somewhat watchful and guarded. Teamwork looks polite and the relationship positive but superficial. This is where it is critical for you to assure that each important start-up activity is accomplished in order for the energy of the team to move past defining goals, relationships, and boundaries and into the work itself. When the critical start-up questions are left unanswered, team energy gets stuck trying to clarify what is expected.

Later, as the team goes through some storming and feeling out of what the real agreements will be, you may need more emphasis on the area of accountabilities, and you may need to emphasize coaching in your leadership responsibilities. At this time, team members are negotiating for power, and determining the norms of how team members will work together. If your fitness sessions help surface issues and make agreements for behaviors, the team will drain off less energy feeling stuck, managing conflicts, or opting out of commitment to team activities.

Has your team worked together to iron out many of the understandings talked about herein? If so, they have grown in their ability to handle problems creatively and flexibly. They are likely to feel more satisfaction and cohesion, and renewed commitment to teamwork. Now your challenge is to get out of the way and let the team do the planning. You'll be amazed at their creative ideas for going beyond the covers of this book into the unlimited ways to improve and invent better ways to work together. Your team is fit! Together you and they can do it! Enjoy!

But it's *still* not over. When your team gets new members (the direction of the organization changes—leadership changes), the team may need redefinition. At this time, revisiting some of the basics you hammered out in team start-up can help tighten up or redirect team activities and keep members from feeling out of control.

Some teams also fall into bad habits or slip on implementing and sustaining team agreements. To rejuvenate or renew your team, it usually is helpful to focus on the customer and the mission and not on the internal workings of the team.

By now, your own experience will lead you on fitness adventures we have not thought of yet. Let us know what works!

Planning an Off-Site Team Fitness Session

How do you build commitment to your team?

The more people you involve in defining your direction and strategy, your goals, and values, the greater the commitment.

It is useful to spend some quality time away from the workplace to do this. There are some important basic decisions that go into the planning for a team-fitness session. Bad decisions here, such as those about who attends, could sidetrack the entire process. Also, many decisions (for example, those around the physical layout and equipment or the logistics) can be made in advance, thus freeing you to concentrate on the work at hand after you are in the session.

Why go off-site?

You are looking for creativity, some good hard thinking and analysis, and for building a spirit of camaraderie, support, and trust. Telephone messages and the urge to check your in-basket are too great when you are in proximity to your desk. It also is harder to raise your sights from the daily problems and deadlines. Going away signals that this is a different, special kind of meeting, not a regular meeting.

And it signals your commitment to build your team. It tells people you believe in this process enough to commit time and money to doing it.

The first decision you need to make is: Who attends?

All of the key players should be there. If someone cannot attend, you might consider rescheduling when all can attend.

You may start with your top management team to achieve clarity and set overall direction before you include everyone. We did a fitness session with a regional financial institution, going off-site with the key administrative office staff and each branch manager. This group determined the vision, the mission, and the major goals of the organization.

One month later we brought together the whole staff (60+), everyone in the organization for an overnight fitness session to work out problems and to develop plans to implement the new mission, vision, and goals. They closed down the offices, except for temporary help to answer the telephone. That act alone demonstrated to everyone that management was committed to their direction and believed that each person was important in carrying out the organization's mission. It also helped ensure that the necessary management support for actions would be there when it was needed.

Where should you go?

There are many good choices. We have conducted fitness sessions in condos in the mountains and by the ocean. We have used church rooms, other corporate offices, hotel suites, rustic church camps, and, of course, elegant resorts with candle-lit dinners. Although we prefer going off-site, we have held some good sessions by simply going to a different part of the facility.

If you are going overnight, try to choose a place without a lot of outside activity or stimulation. We prefer more isolation where there aren't a lot of other people or groups so that work can be focused on your own team needs.

The room you work in must be large enough to accommodate everyone comfortably. You need tables where people can write and see everyone else in the room. We prefer round tables to encourage participation and minimize any hierarchy that may exist. Windows and comfort are important in ensuring people can be creative and stay focused. For one session, we had to call seven hotels before we found one with windows and the room size we needed. It rained the entire time we were there, but the windows somehow kept us in touch with the world and provided the retreat feeling we needed.

A setting with gardens or natural scenery can help people recharge on their breaks and lunch hours. Select the setting that fits your budget and audience, and that somehow helps people get in the proper frame of mind.

What equipment do we need?

Aside from tables and chairs, you need at least two flip charts. One is for the issue you are discussing; the other is for ideas that come up that need to be dealt with, but don't pertain directly to the work you are doing, or cannot be decided by the group you have assembled. If small groups are working part of the time, you may wish to have a flip chart available for each group. See Appendix G.

We frequently use a VCR and monitor for videotapes. Videos often bring in the best thinking of the outside world or provide a laugh break that keeps people energized.

What do we do in off-work time on an overnight?

You can spend the time informally with no agenda or you can continue to work, if people are on a roll.

If you have no agenda, you can play games, such as poker or bridge. Trivial Pursuit® and Pictionary® are good for teams and are games that encourage individuals to trust each other . We also have used outward bound activities, not river rafting, or rappelling down cliffs, but physical team problem-solving activities.

Often we show videotapes in this time, stopping them frequently to discuss application to the business. This also is a good time for self-understanding activities (found in Part 3.)

A lot of good team-building gets done over cards or during informal evening talk sessions. Some people will drift off to bed. Others will stay up until the wee hours in the common room and talk. That is often appropriate.

How long should the session last?

One-half day is better than nothing. Two or three half days spread out over a month will work, too. Session length should be determined by the needs of the team and your particular situation. An overnight is optimal because of the concentrated work time and social time together.

What should be on the agenda?

Use your team to plan the agenda. Check with your Fitness Meter for needs and use Part 3 for exercise ideas.

How often should we go off-site?

Much depends on what kind of team you are. Many ongoing teams do a full-fledged overnight off-site team strategy session once a year. Follow-up on action plans should occur monthly, at minimum, with perhaps a half-day session off-site (but close to home) every quarter to see how things are going.

The team should monitor itself on contracts made with individuals and should periodically process check to determine how well it is functioning. Are we still headed in the direction we want to go? What is getting in our way? How can we overcome these obstacles? These are all potential subjects for a quarterly review.

When you are experienced, consider including the stakeholders, customers, suppliers, and other interested parties as a reality check for the thinking of the team.

How should we end the session?

Evaluate what you did. Review all the discussions and decisions. Build and agree on an action plan. Plan time for follow-up. Allow each person to make a statement on the session, something like: "What was most important to me." Celebrate progress.

Roles and Tasks of a Facilitator

Fit teams frequently use a designated facilitator—someone who steps aside from the content and concentrates on the process the team is using to do its work. This role can be shared. A good time to facilitate for your team is when they take up a topic on which you have no really strong feelings. This helps you to remain neutral and focus more on the process.

Following are some tips on how to help your team as a facilitator:*

1. Lead by example and make suggestions that help others do this also.

   • Participate without dominating.

   • Be supportive of other team members' thinking.

   • Accept diverse views.

   • Listen actively to others' views.

   • Don't become defensive.

2. Lead the group in accomplishing the task.

   • Establish norms of participation by all members.

   • Promote interaction.

*Adapted from material developed by Dr. Mary Bendalow, Principal, Communi-Consultants, Conifer, Colorado.

- Maintain the group's direction and agenda.

- Promote discussion while maintaining control.

- Keep the discussion focused and on track, without squelching lively debate.

- Summarize major points.

3. Provide for maintenance of positive team relationships.

- Surface and mediate underlying conflicts and issues. (For example, if someone keeps arguing about a topic you think is finished, there probably is something else going on for that person. Ask questions.).

- Gatekeep. Ask for each person's opinion.

- Encourage quiet people without embarrassing.

- Discourage overtalkers and dominant people.

- Refocus wandering discussion by summarizing and restating the goal.

- Promote a climate of openness and acceptance.

- Monitor peoples' reactions.

4. Acknowledge that you are wearing three or more hats, playing different roles—discussion leader, participant, and neutral facilitator. Be flexible and be prepared to change hats.

5. Maintain a good sense of humor and go with the flow, when necessary.

Use of Flip Charts

The ideas, plans, and decisions recorded on the flip chart provide a permanent record of the meeting which can later be transcribed as minutes, notes, or action plans.

Some suggestions for using flip charts follow:

1. Use marking pens that are dark enough for everyone to see.

2. List the topic under discussion at the top of the page.

3. As each person finishes a point, ask him or her to summarize it and record their summary on the flip chart.

4. If the idea is special to the group or to the person, but irrelevant to the topic under discussion, record it on a second flip chart. You can label this, "Don't Forget" or "Other Issues" or "Parking Lot."

5. If you, the leader, summarize or shorten the person's contribution, check with that person to determine your accuracy. "Is this what you meant? Does this capture your idea?"

The advantages of using the flip chart are

• All contributions are noted.

• No information is lost.

- Focus is on the idea, not the person who said it.

- People speak to the point, reducing digressions.

- People stay involved in and focused on the topic.

Post all flip charts on the wall. Refer to them as you go through your session. The posted flip charts also serve to remind people of what they have accomplished.

What do you do with the alternate flip chart? We use it to prioritize the issues that arise. Is this something to deal with here? Is this a decision/issue we in this room can deal with/change? With limited time, which of these topics do you want to talk about?

Return to this chart later to see if anything has been missed or to determine the direction of the agenda. "Have we covered this point, or should we address it now?" Keep all flip charts and transcribe as minutes of your meetings. Share with team members following the meeting.

Bibliography

Bell, C. "Turning Customers Into Partners." *At Work,* March–April 1993, 19.

Bendalow, M. Principal, Communi-Consultants, Conifer, Colorado.

Berry L. L., D. R. Bennett, and C. W. Brown. *Service Quality: Profit Strategy for Financial Institutions.* Homewood, Ill.: Dow Jones-Irwin, 1989.

Berry, L. L., V. A. Zeithami, and A. Parasuraman. "Quality Counts in Services, Too." *Business Horizons,* May–June 1985, 44–52.

Brokaw, L. "The Truth about Start-ups". *Inc.,* March 1993, 56–57.

Burnside, J. *Letting Go.* General Electric Company, 1992.

Carlzon, J. *Moments of Truth.* New York: Harper and Row, 1987.

Chapman, C. R., and D. Morrison. *New York Times,* June 20, 1991.

Hardaker, M., and B. K. Ward. "Getting Things Done: How to Make a Team Work." *Harvard Business Review,* November–December 1987, 112–119.

Hurst, D. K. "Of Boxes and Bubbles and Effective Management." *Harvard Business Review,* May–June 1984, 78.

Isgar, T. *Ten Minute Team.* Boulder, Colo.: Seluera Press, 1989.

Keidel, R. W. "Baseball, Football, and Basketball: Models for Business." *Organizational Dynamics,* Winter 1984, 5–18.

Larson, C. and F. LaFasto. *Team Effectiveness.* Newbury Park, Calif.: Sage Publishing, 1991.

McDonald, P. "The Huddle System". *Inc.,* October 1992, 25.

Petrock, F. "Just Tell Us What It Is You Want." *Business Month,* December 1989, 86.

Quick, J. "Crafting Organizational Culture: Herb's Hand at Southwest Airlines." *Organizational Dynamics,* Winter 1993, 45–56.

Schilder, J. "Work Teams Boost Productivity." *Personnel Journal,* February 1992, 67–71.

Solomon, J. "Fall of the Dinosaurs." *Newsweek,* February 8, 1993, 42–44.

Index

A

Access, 43, 45
Accountability, xv, 186
  assessment of, 17, 22, 23
  critical success factors in,
    219–20
  definition of 7, 185
  establishing priorities in, 211–12
  factors that influence, 7
  focus on, and team fitness, 7
  implementation planning in,
    213–16
  individual contracting in, 203–5
  negotiating ground rules in,
    201–2
  operating agreements in, 7,
    196–200
  planning for, 25
  project planning in, 206
  stakeholder support in, 217–18
  team responsibility in, 207–10
  values and beliefs in, 7, 188–89,
    193, 194–95
Agenda for off-site team meeting
  234
Assurance, 53

B

Balance, determining, for team,
  167–69
Baseball, lessons to be learned
  from, 159
Basketball, lessons to be learned
  from, 160–61
Behavior
  creative versus concrete, 167–69
  individual, 146–51
  self-, 147, 151
  task, 147, 149
  types of team, 147
Boss, characteristics of best, 174–75
Bottom-up goal setting, 118–20

C

Chartering, 5, 82–83
  of long-term or ongoing teem,
    89–91
  of new team, 84–88
Commitment, building team, 231
Communication, 43, 45
Competence, 43, 44
Consensus, 154

Consensus decision making, 152–56
Continuous improvement, 165–66
Contracting, individual, 203–5
Courtesy, 43–45, 45
Creativity, on team, 167–69
Credibility, 43, 45
Critical success factors, 219–20
Cultural observation, 181–83
Culture audit, 177–80
Customer
    interview format for external, 64–66
    interview format for internal, 62–63
Customer feedback and measures, 39–40
Customer focus, xv, 29
    assessment of, 14, 19, 23
    customer feedback and measures in, 39–40
    customer identification in, 4, 29, 31–36
        primary, 34–36
    customer needs and expectations in, 37–38, 46–47
    customer priorities in, 41–45
    definition of, 4, 29
    factors in, 4, 29
    focus groups in, 60–66
    judging actions in, 76–77
    moments of truth in, 48–54
    planning for, 24
    priorities in, 41–45
    site visits in, 55–59
    surveys in, 67–72
    tracking work in, 73–75
Customer identification, 4, 29, 31–36
    primary, 34–36
Customer needs and expectations, 4, 29, 37–38
Customer priorities, 41–45
Customer site visits, 55–59

D

Direction, 79
    assessment of, 15, 20, 23
    chartering in, 82–91
    definitions in, 5, 79
    factors in, 5
    goals and objectives in, 112–26
    mission statements in, 102–11
    planning for, 24
    visioning in, 92–101

E

Empathy, 53
External customers, interview format for, 64–66

F

Facilitator, roles and tasks of, 235–36
Flip charts, 237–38
Focus groups
    interview format for external customers, 64–66
    interview format for internal customers, 62–63
Football, lessons to be learned from, 160

G

General Electric's Business Information Center (Albany, New York), xvi
Global competition, 11
Goals and objectives, 5, 112–13
    bottom-up, 118–20
    definition of, 112
    priority in, 121–26
    top-down, 114–17
Ground rules, negotiation of, 201–2

H

Huddle system, 163
Hypergrowth companies, and team start-ups, 12

I

Implementation planning, 7, 213–16
Independence/interdependence needs, 157–61
In-depth introductions, 130–35
Individual behaviors, 146–51
Individual contracting, 203–5
Internal customers, interview format for, 62–63
Interview format
    for external customers, 64–66
    for internal customers, 62–63
Interview questions, for customer site visits, 58

J

Johnsonville Foods, 90

L

Leadership transition meeting, 170–73
Leasing company, sample vision, mission, and goals for, 80
"Lobby lizard" approach, 48
Longstreet, John, 48
Long-term team chartering meeting, 89–91

M

Maintenance behaviors, 147, 150
Marquette University Center for the Study of Entrepreneurship, 12

Mission, 5
Mission statements, 102–4
    short, 108–11
Moments of truth, 48–54

N

Negotiation of ground rules, 201–2
Northern Telecom (Morrisville factory), 90

O

Objectives. *See* Goals and objectives
Off-site team fitness session, planning, 231–34
One-day visioning meeting, 94–96
Ongoing team chartering meeting, 89–91
Operating agreements, 7, 196–200
Organization, 176
    culture audit, 177–80
    culture observation, 181–83

P

Primary customer identification, 34–36
Priorities
    customer, 41–45
    establishing, 211–12
    goal setting in, 121–26
Process check, 165–66
Project planning, 7, 206
Protocol for site visits, 57

R

Reliability, 43, 53
Responsiveness, 43, 44, 53
Reynolds, Paul, 12

S

Security, 43–45, 45
Self behaviors, 147, 151
Self-directed teams, 90
Service firm, sample survey for, 70–72
Service quality, dimensions of, 43–45, 53–54
Site visits, customer, 55–59
Sports, lessons to be learned from, 159–61
Stakeholder support, 217–18
Steelcase, 90
Surveys, 67–72

T

Tangibles, 43, 45, 53
Task behaviors, 147, 149
Team(s), 142
    accountability in, xv
    assessing responsibility on, 207–10
    assessing strengths and needs of, 13–23
    beginning with existing, 227–28
    behavior on, 147
    building commitment, 231
    characteristics of effective, 11–12, 145
    chartering of new, 84–88
    consensus decision making on, 152–56
    creativity versus concrete behavior in, 167–69
    customer focus in, xv
    direction of, xv
    independence/interdependence needs in, 157–61
    in-depth introduction of members, 130–35
    individual behaviors in, 146–51
    leadership of, 170–75
    performance of, xv
    self-directed, 90
    starting up new, 225–26
    time management in, 229–30
    types of, 223–24
    understanding in, xv
Team fitness analysis, 23
    accountability in, 7, 17, 22, 25
    customer focus in, 4, 14, 19, 24
    direction in, 4, 15, 20, 24
    schedule for, 26
    scoring of, 18–22
    understanding in, 6, 16, 21, 24–25
Ten-minute team process, 162–64
Time management, 139–41, 229–30
Top-down goals and objectives, 114–17
Tracking work exercise, 73–75

U

Understanding, xv, 43, 45, 127–28
    analysis of fitness assessment scores for, 23
    assessment of, 16, 21
    definition of, 6
    factors in, 6
    in-depth introductions in, 130–35
    organization, 176–83
    planning for, 24–25

self and others, 129–41
sharing in, 136–38
team, 142–75
time management in, 139–41

V

Values
   and accountability, 7, 188–89,
      193, 194–95
   in driving business, 194
Values statements, 193

Visioning, 92–93
   creating with pictures, 99–101
   one-day meeting, 94–96
   warm-up, 97–98

W

Warm-up visioning, 97–98
Weighted pairs in establishing goal
      priority, 124, 126
Work flow, tracking of, 73–75
Work group, team versus, 143–45